CYBER SECURITY

Comprehensive Beginners Guide to Learn the Basics and Effective Methods of Cyber Security

Brian Walker

© Copyright 2019 - All rights reserved.

The content contained within this book may not be reproduced, duplicated or transmitted without direct written permission from the author or the publisher.

Under no circumstances will any blame or legal responsibility be held against the publisher, or author, for any damages, reparation, or monetary loss due to the information contained within this book. Either directly or indirectly.

Legal Notice:

This book is copyright protected. This book is only for personal use. You cannot amend, distribute, sell, use, quote or paraphrase any part, or the content within this book, without the consent of the author or publisher.

Disclaimer Notice:

Please note the information contained within this document is for educational and entertainment purposes only. All effort has been executed to present accurate, up to date, and reliable, complete information. No warranties of any kind are declared or implied. Readers acknowledge that the author is not engaging in the rendering of legal, financial, medical or professional advice. The content within this book has been derived from various sources. Please consult a licensed professional before attempting any techniques outlined in this book.

By reading this document, the reader agrees that under no circumstances is the author responsible for any losses, direct or indirect, which are incurred as a result of the use of information contained within this document, including, but not limited to, — errors, omissions, or inaccuracies.

Table of Contents

Introduction 1

Chapter 1: Fundamentals in Cyber Security 9

    The Cyberspace Concept 10

    Connectivity's Benefits 14

    Understanding Cyber Security 16

Chapter 2: Importance of Cyber Security 17

    Cost Considerations 19

    The Business of Security 20

    No One Is Safe 20

    Smarter Hackers 22

    Expanding the Internet of Things 23

    Evolution of Hacking Equipment, Tools, and Techniques 26

    Growing Demand for Data Access 27

    Regulations 27

    Protecting Yourself from Cyber Attacks 28

Chapter 3: Notable Security Breaches 30
    Yahoo 31
    Marriott International 32
    Home Depot 34
    JP Morgan Chase 34
    Google 35
    Uber 36
    Target 37
    Anthem 38
    Sony – PlayStation 39
    Sony Pictures 39
    Adobe 41
    Stuxnet 41
    RSA Security 42
    Heartland Payment Systems 43
    eBay 44
    US Office of Personnel Management (OPM) 45
    Equifax 46
    Adult Friend Finder 46
    VeriSign 47
    TJX Companies Inc. 48
    Cambridge Analytica 48
    Facebook 49

Chapter 4: Data Encryption 51

Cryptography in Information Security 51

Asymmetric Encryption 53

Symmetric Encryption 55

Comparing Symmetric and Asymmetric Encryption 57

The Role of Data Encryption 57

Challenges in Implementing Encryption Protocols 61

Encryption Mistakes That Leave You Exposed 63

Debunking Myths About Data Encryption 69

Chapter 5: Initiating Breach Protocol 75

Mitigating Future Attacks 80

Chapter 6: Preventing Cyber Attacks 86

Types of Cyber Attacks 86

How to Protect Your Business 88

Threat Identification 89

Expect an Attack 90

Employee Management 90

Two-Factor Authentication 91

System Audits 92

Signing Off Policies 93

Insurance Policy 93

Cyberattack Resilience 94

Software Updates 94

Penetration Testing 95

The Need for Proper Training 95

Protect Your Emails 96
Virtual Private Network (VPN) 96
Disaster Management Plan 97
Privileged User Access 97
DDoS Protection 98
Gateway Layer Protection 99
Personal Devices 99
Additional Protection for Critical Operations 99
State of the Business Address 100
Endpoint Protection 100
Make Cyber Security Everyone's Prerogative 101

Chapter 7: General Data Protection Regulation (GDPR) 102
Impact of GDPR on Governments 103
Impact of GDPR on Research 107
Impact of GDPR on Learning Institutions 109
Impact of GDPR on Consumers 112
Impact of GDPR on Businesses 114

Chapter 8: Embracing the Future of Cyber Security 117
Future Cyber Threat Assessment 118
Consequences for the Average User 120
Protecting the Internet of Things 121
Big Data 122
Stringent Regulations 124
Quantum Computing 125
Artificial Intelligence 125

Ransomware 126
Digital Transformation 128
Nation-State Attacks 129
Data Weaponization 129
Satellite Attacks 130

Conclusion **132**

References **138**

Introduction

The average human operates on autopilot every day. There are actions and activities that we perform from the moment we wake up to the time we retire to bed in the evening that have become a part of us. We just subconsciously perform these actions. Without doing certain activities, one probably cannot live a happy and fulfilling life. One might not even live at all and end up becoming a dud in society. Yet, we get through these actions without thinking. Most of these tasks are things we have learned to do over the years, either out of necessity or as a requirement.

Think about it. After awakening, one of the first five things most people do is check their phones. This might not have been the case in the year 1995, but in 2019, it is a different story altogether. This is an adaptation; we have learned to adapt to certain changes in the environment we live in, especially within the world of technology.

Most people wake up, go to the bathroom, get ready for their daily routine, and lock the door behind them after they leave. Perhaps within the first few minutes of clarity when they arrive at their desk and sip their favorite beverage, they will notice they may have missed something. That's the moment you realize everything in your schedule runs on autopilot.

Most things in your daily routine that run on autopilot are done so out of logic. It makes sense to lock the door when you leave for work as a security measure. You check your phone when you wake up to see if you have received any important notifications while you were asleep, which might influence your day ahead. You freshen up before you leave the house. All of these are logical actions. Even when you get inside your car, you put on your seatbelt, not because you will get into an accident, but because it is logical to do so; the seatbelt might protect you in the unlikely event that you are involved in a car accident.

The basic understanding behind this chain of events is that, in life, there are dangers all around you. You might never see them coming, and some may not be very frequent, but in hindsight, you are always aware of a risk. To mitigate these dangers, you learn to logically make some changes in life, in your routine, and at times, also for the people around you. The same mechanisms you learn in order to maneuver through life safely and successfully are the ones you teach your children so that they too can have a chance at succeeding in life.

Fast forward to an important aspect in your life today and what some would even consider a prerequisite: the internet. You have plans in place to deal with or mitigate most risks you are exposed to in life, but are you ready to do the same for your internet life?

Most people today have a second life online. Whether as an individual or a company, you need an internet presence for various reasons. Billions of people are connected to the internet through all sorts of devices. Today, access to the internet is almost classified as a basic need, alongside food, clothing, and shelter. It's almost inconceivable to imagine a world without the internet. Most people's lives are thrown into disarray in the event of an internet outage; the outbursts on social media whenever one of the social media platforms is inaccessible is proof of this concept.

The fact is, your connection to the internet is important and probably one of the reasons why you stay relevant today. You interact with the rest of the world when you perform tasks like connecting to a wireless network, clicking on a link, accessing an application or a website, interacting via email, purchasing items online, publishing an article online, interacting on social media accounts, and so forth.

These days, you even have gadgets connected to your phone and other devices that monitor your heartbeat, such that even when you are miles away, your loved ones can keep an eye on your health and help you stay on course. Oh, the glorious marvels of the internet!

Companies are working hard to push different projects online in a bid to make work easier. If you are ever in doubt, speak to an accountant. You do not have to spend time going through physical receipts and thinking about accounting formulas when all you really need to do is take a photo of your receipt, and QuickBooks will do the rest, presenting you with a monthly accounting report. You can connect your PayPal account or a bank account with QuickBooks and receive a complete financial report at the end of whichever trading period you fancy. What does this mean for the average user? Well, it means you needn't pay an accountant to prepare your finances. You may, however, need a financial advisor to help you understand your monetary position.

The internet and technology are about so much more than accounting. In recent times, the fiscal market is under siege from cryptocurrency. Almost everyone is aware of the upheavals that Bitcoin and other altcoins have presented. Other than fronting as alternative currencies to conventional fiat currency, most cryptocurrency platforms are actually development platforms for different projects. The decentralized element of cryptocurrency aims to do away with the middlemen in the financial markets, connecting users to their desired services and service providers directly.

Away from the financial markets, the internet of things (IoT) is thriving, embraced by many sectors in the world. Surgeons can now perform very delicate operations with the help of technological gadgets that never would have been thought possible a few years ago (Friedman, Metzler, Detmer, Selzer, & Meara, 2012). Companies have come to the fore, challenging the status quo and succeeding doing so. Companies like Uber are thriving in the taxi industry without owning taxis. Airbnb is running one of the biggest hospitality operations in the world without owning any property.

This is merely the tip of the iceberg when looking at the prospects of the internet.

At the heart of all these amazing developments is data. All these systems need some form of data; without it, they would be no more than skeletons. Data is the blueprint upon which these systems derive their lives. Considering the amount of data needed and harvested by the systems we interact with on a daily basis, you can only imagine the value of internet data. With all the right information, someone can create a similar but alternate identity of you while living a normal life in a different part of the world. Identity theft is not a new phenomenon.

The most important question at this juncture, therefore, is whether we should worry about all this data about us and our lives. Companies are paying tidy sums to access your data. Others are going about it through unscrupulous means. However, the common denominator is your data and gaining access to it. From companies to governments and other organizations, everyone is out to obtain your data for different reasons. From the very moment you obtain a device that can collect some form of information about you, you join an intricate and interconnected electronic system. While this system largely works for you, it almost certainly will also work against you. All the entities that are legally entitled to accessing your data might use it to try and understand you better, tailoring their services to suit your needs. On the other hand, this data also allows them to manipulate you into doing something specific. They influence your logic. You might feel you purchased something online because you needed it, but upon careful analysis, you realize you were coerced into the purchase through subtle mind games.

On the other side of the data access spectrum are hackers. Hackers are criminals, for lack of a better word. Of course we also have ethical hackers (Gupta, 2019), who are guys that hack systems to determine their vulnerability and advise companies and entities on how to bolster their security apparatus (talk about setting a thief to catch a thief).

The meaning of a hacker is relative. Mention of the word hacking almost always elicits negative responses from individuals. However, depending on the context, a hacker is not always the bad guy. By definition, a hacker is an investigator. They learn the finer details about a programmable system and how to circumvent the capabilities of these systems. The difference between a hacker and any other person who might also have access to the same programmable system is that, while most people only learn the basics (or what is spoon-fed to them), a hacker takes time to learn more than what everyone else sees. If they suspect a vulnerability, they commit time and other resources to exploit it. The more a hacker knows about a system, the better for them.

Today, cyber criminals are commonly referred to as hackers, black hat hackers, attackers, or crackers. While most of their attacks are centered around stealing money from their victims, some hackers also go about their crimes just because they can. The satisfaction of accessing some of the most protected networks and systems in the world gives such hackers bragging rights and respect within the hacking world. Other than financial gains, there also exist hacktivists, who are individuals who attack systems for an ideological cause (Vegh, 2002).

There are so many reasons why someone might be interested in hacking your systems. Each day, hackers come up with new methods of obtaining important and privileged information about you. This information can be obtained willingly or not. Considering the fact that most companies that are hacked barely disclose the real extent of the damage, some people believe the aftermath of a well-orchestrated aftermath could be more expensive than the cost of some natural disasters, and all this without causing anyone physical harm.

The internet might be a good place considering how resourceful it is, but at the same time, it is the murkiest place on earth. Each time you're online, there is always someone lurking around who is ready to pounce when you least expect it.

It doesn't matter who you are; the dangers of the internet can befall anyone, whether you are the President of the US or an ordinary citizen. One of the most important things you should understand about cyber security is that the idea of zero risk is a myth. Anyone who tries to convince you that your interaction with them online carries zero risk is selling you a flat out lie. Risks are found everywhere online. Every time you click on a link, there is a risk that it might have been hijacked by hackers prior to your access. What we must learn to do is identify these attacks and try to prevent them from taking place. Protecting yourself, your networks, and your devices is the most important thing you can do - at least from your end. Preventing cyber attacks is an all-inclusive process in which each individual who needs access to the internet must pull their weight.

Do not think about cyber security as a sole obligation of security companies, as you as an individual also have a role to play in it. Your devices can be inadvertently used to hack into a very secure system, leaving you in a lot of trouble.

Considering the nature of losses that companies deal with in the aftermath of a cyber attack (as you will learn later on in this book), you have to play your part diligently. Just as you lock your door and double check that it's locked for security reasons when you leave your house in the morning, you should also take the necessary precautions to protect your internet access.

You never know who is watching.

Chapter 1

Fundamentals in Cyber Security

Governments, companies, and individuals make cyber security a primary concern. We cannot ignore the stark reality we face today. Cyber security is important, yet it is very difficult to achieve. There are so many dynamics at play that complicate the nature of cyber security, yet we must strive to maintain a balance in the face of a continually evolving cyber ecosystem. The future of cyber security depends on what we do about it today.

Most vulnerabilities occur because the relevant parties barely understand the fundamentals of cyber security. This lack of understanding breeds another problem, and this is an exaggeration of perceived concerns. Given the allure of political and commercial incentives, we must return to the basics to understand the fundamentals of cyber security, and from there, we should then channel our efforts in the right direction.

The Cyberspace Concept

Cyber security is about cyberspace. Cyberspace refers to an interactive space comprising of digital networks that collect, store, and manipulate information to facilitate different forms of communication. Therefore, cyberspace includes the internet and a host of systems that support the internet's services, infrastructure, and participants (Hunter & Huntert, 2003; Kohl, 2015).

To meet its functional objectives, cyberspace is a multi-layered platform that is made up of the following:

Information – Information is what people seek in cyberspace. From financial transactions, texts, and all forms of media and social media posts, people go online to interact with one another regarding these things. This information is stored in different media, including the private and public cloud, ready for retrieval as soon as the user requests it. Even after access, the information is still stored in databases across the world and can be manipulated or modified to suit the creator or the audience's needs.

Physical foundations – The physical foundations of cyberspace include satellites, submarine cables, land cables, and anything else that provides a pathway for communication. These are the transmission modules through which communication is permitted. They also include routers, which ensure the destined recipient can access the relayed information (and hopefully, no one else).

People – We the people are the producers and consumers of information shared in the cyberspace. We also build all the logical and physical elements of cyberspace.

Logical building blocks – These are the operating systems, applications, and web browsers that allow us to interact with the physical foundations and access information online.

These layers make up the cyberspace. We need them to work hand in hand every day to allow us access to the internet and to facilitate our desire to meet our objectives. An efficient cyberspace is reliable. It works just as well as an efficient healthcare, transportation, or energy sector. Most people depend on cyberspace and its efficiency. However, as happens with any system, increased dependency always breeds challenges such as disruption. Whether it is intentional or by accident, disruption has dire costs

It is very easy to confuse the internet or the web for cyberspace. In digital communications, these are overlapping systems, but they are not the same thing. The mention of cyber security almost always has people thinking about the vulnerabilities of the devices, computers, or websites that they access frequently. Cyberspace, however, is much bigger than that. Cyberspace is the culmination of digital networks all over the world. Cyberspace includes legacy communication protocols and networks that are so isolated you cannot access them through the internet. What most people are aware of and have access to is the internet protocol (IP) network. This is by far just a tip of the iceberg and the smallest possible component of cyberspace. The fact that the IP network is one of the most widely used and popular communication platforms can easily mislead you to believe it is all there is to cyberspace.

Within the internet, we have the web. The web refers to the pages we can access through our web browsers. The terms "web" and "internet" are often used interchangeably, but they are actually not the same thing. Most discussions about cyber security are centered around securing the internet, because this is where most communication takes place on a global scale.

For the four layers of cyberspace to work in tandem and support the desire for efficiency, they must possess three important characteristics: storage, speed, and connectivity. These three characteristics account for every aspect of cyberspace. The digital environment experiences different aspects of our interaction, and whether positive or negative, it relies on these three things.

The best possible understanding of cyberspace and cyber security starts by learning about the core layers of cyberspace, their characteristics, and studying their role in the stability and safety of the digital space.

- **Storage** - Connectivity and speed are two of the most important characteristics of cyberspace. Before we get to those, however, let's look at storage. Without the right storage facilities, speed and connectivity would be useless. Think about it - what benefit does it serve you to have all the speed and connectivity in the world when you can't store resources to access them whenever you need to?

Hard drives keep increasing in size. People want them smaller in physical size, but gigantic in their handling capacity. It might be difficult for most people to imagine this, but there was a time when floppy diskettes with a few kilobytes of space was all you ever needed. This is currently dwarfed by all the terabytes of space we have access to - and the storage potential will only keep growing.

Storage is not just about capacity. Storage is underpinned by performance. The storage device must meet certain input/output speed requirements for compatibility with some devices. This explains why you might copy a file faster across a certain operating system, but copying the same file might be slower on another.

- **Speed** - Cyberspace evolves faster than the physical world does. Whatever is new today might be out of date in a week. This dynamic change is responsible for the many advancements we enjoy today. The processing power of computers is responsible for speed. As the computers get more powerful, you're able to perform more tasks in an infinitely short time. In the digital world, speed is everything. You get more hits if your website loads in under three seconds; the attention span of most users today is that short. Anything more than three seconds, and the user will feel disheartened, seeking alternatives. If they open another tab, chances are high that in three minutes, they will have accessed more than ten tabs and probably will have forgotten about the first tab they opened, which did not load as fast as they expected it to.

- **Connectivity** - At least 40 percent of the global population has access to the internet through smartphones, tablets, personal computers, and laptops. Besides these traditional forms, the internet of things introduces more access points to the internet through sensors embedded in different tools, appliances, and equipment you interact with at work, home, school, and so forth. This means that, aside from the basic elements of connectivity, there are billions of other access points to the internet that we use from time to time.

Connectivity's Benefits

The positive network effect of increased connectivity through all these devices helps to generate more benefits and value than the perceived individual parts working independently. The more devices we have connected to the internet, the more information is collected and shared. As the network grows, therefore, so does its value - especially in the value of data held.

There are so many benefits of connectivity. You can email someone in a remote part of the world, and they're able to respond in seconds. Social networks keep burgeoning over time, and the wider their reach, the more valuable the networks are. Through wider connectivity, it is easier to identify and study trends and make predictions based on analysis. This explains why data analysis is currently one of the most lucrative fields that exist.

Efficient connectivity also helps to bridge the distance challenge behind communication. Messages can be shared reliably all over the world. Companies today are implementing remote working spaces through which their employees can work from home and still contribute to the business objectives (Meredith, 2005). This removes the struggle of wasting a lot of time in traffic. At the same time, hackers also rely on the connectivity of the internet. It works just as well for them as it works for your good deeds.

The ramifications of connectivity, storage, and speed working together are far-reaching. However, there are two important deductions that we can get from this. First, the digital world in which we live depends on digital technologies, and in most cases, the nature of dependency is not immediately apparent. Most digital communication is facilitated by the internet. Other industries that are equally important to the global economy, like the food and transportation industries, also rely on the internet to bolster their efficiency and reduce the inherent transaction costs. Therefore, the internet is the central nervous system of the global economy, and it will only keep growing to meet increasing demands.

Secondly, all technology is dual-use (Fischer, 2005). The benefits that you enjoy from an efficient network are the same benefits that a hacker needs to exploit that network. Most policy makers tend to ignore the dual-use nature of technology, and in the process, they come up with perceived solutions to societal concerns which breed more problems in the long run.

Understanding Cyber Security

The cyberspace characteristics discussed above work together to create threats in the same way they create amazing opportunities. As the business world keeps growing, the threats get more sophisticated and the costs of remediation even higher. Cyber security is about protecting the availability, integrity, and confidentiality of information.

It's not easy to protect networks and devices, because you need protection against all different kinds of attacks, some of which you are not even aware. The hacker, on the other hand, only needs one vulnerability to exploit. Risk assessment is important in cyber security. However, it's also becoming difficult to assess risks effectively, because the scope of attack keeps growing with time. Back in the day, hackers only needed to hack computers. Today, there are many devices connected to the internet, and most of them are vulnerable. The moment that one such device is exploited, any network it's connected to is no longer safe and neither are the devices connected to that network.

Modern economies need software for functionality. Think about communication networks, transportation, national security, and energy networks. All these networks need technology to function and enable us to live a normal and satisfying life. It's not easy to build good software. After all, it's only good when it's used for the right purpose. That same software can also be used by hackers for nefarious reasons. Vulnerabilities present in computer systems and networks create a risky situation for information access, government secrets, intellectual property, and so forth. The very fabric of the internet is not safe.

Chapter 2

Importance of Cyber Security

The month of October gets people excited for a few different reasons. While some are looking forward to Oktoberfest, tech fellows look forward to Cyber Security Month.[1] This is usually the time when discussions about cyber security, conventions, and so on take precedence. It does not mean that these discussions don't take place throughout the year, either. The importance of cyber security is such that you cannot ignore it at any time.

Technology has taken over the way we lead our lives today. From professional networking to interactions and collaboration on work documents, we rely on technology to get so much done. The risk of compromise for these connections is very high, and the prospective losses are equally higher.

People often look at cyber security risks for big and small businesses and assume that they are the only targets for

---

[1] Cyber Security Month https://cybersecuritymonth.eu

cyberattacks. They might be the main targets, considering the amount of data that they collect and store on their servers, but individual users are just as vulnerable to attacks. As long as you connect to the internet through any device, no one is too small or too big to suffer a cyberattack.

Take the UK, for example; the Cyber Security Breaches Survey[2] reported that in 2017, almost 43 percent of businesses registered in the UK were subject to some sort of cyber breach. As a result of these hacks, the victims lost important files, had their software corrupted, lost systems, lost access to websites, and in some cases, lost assets and intellectual property.

One of the most common attacks today is carried out through impersonation. The attackers impersonate a business and send spamming mail to their clients. These emails are often loaded with malware and viruses. This is the same way phishing attacks are carried out. The Bureau further indicated that, on average, companies end up spending in excess of $3,000 in the wake of these attacks, which can have extremely negative consequences, especially on a small business.

The cost isn't even the biggest problem; you can lose everything. If you do not take the right precautionary measures to protect your

---

[2] 2017 Cyber Security Breaches Report
https://assets.publishing.service.gov.uk/government/uploads/system/uploads/attachment_data/file/609186/Cyber_Security_Breaches_Survey_2017_main_report_PUBLIC.pdf

devices, you may risk jail time in the case that your devices were compromised and used as a proxy through which a bigger attack was carried out. Looking at the risk exposure, it is wise to understand how important cyber security is. Below we go into depth regarding why you need to make cyber security one of your highest priorities.

Cost Considerations

In 2015, Forbes reported that the cyber security market was worth at least $75 billion. At the time, the projections were that this would increase to more than $170 billion by the year 2020[3]. These figures provide you with the most basic understanding of how important it is to focus on cyber security.

From personal digital assets, to governments, to businesses, the demand for the best security measures keeps increasing by the day. In a Cisco report, it was stated that by the year 2020, there will be an insane demand for more than six million cyber security jobs[4]. This is a segment that is growing in leaps and bounds, and it matters to everyone who needs access to the internet.

---

[3] 2017 Cyber Security Breaches Report
https://assets.publishing.service.gov.uk/government/uploads/system/uploads/attachment_data/file/609186/Cyber_Security_Breaches_Survey_2017_main_report_PUBLIC.pdf

[4] Future cyber security job prospects
https://www.forbes.com/sites/stevemorgan/2016/01/02/one-million-cybersecurity-job-openings-in-2016/#2c3b573e27ea

Cyberattacks are very expensive. Businesses have crumbled in the wake of such attacks. Other than the financial risk involved, the reputational and psychological impact that attacks have is tremendous. When your personal data (and in some cases, very intimate data) is stolen, it's difficult to fathom the reputational risks. A lot of individuals have committed suicide when some of their intimate conversations were leaked online. This is truly how expensive cyber attacks can be.

The Business of Security

From individuals to large companies, intellectual property is one of the reasons why people are finding themselves in court battles that could have been avoided. People are leveraging on the opportunities created by the internet of things and developing amazing solutions to today's problems. Something that starts as a hobby might turn into the next Facebook overnight.

As a result, everyone is working towards protecting their interests. For companies, it is an even bigger risk, given that if their resources are exposed, they do not just stand to lose from the data breach, but they also risk a huge settlement to offset the damages to their customers.

No One Is Safe

When you take a defensive driving course, you are not only protecting yourself, but you are protecting every other driver you might cross paths with. The same applies when you fall sick with the flu and decide to stay at home; you protect everyone else by confining the flu to your home rather than spreading it to everyone else between your home and the office. These same principles apply when you're talking about cyber security.

The measures you take to protect your devices will not just keep you safe, but by extension, a lot of people on the internet will stay safe, too. An infected device becomes a host and conduit through which other devices are infected. If your devices are infected, any router you connect to are at risk, especially those that have poor security measures. It follows that all devices connected to that network are also at risk. In a short time, an infection in a personal laptop at the airport might spread to an office block in Manhattan and, through a shared file, spread to New Delhi, Johannesburg, and Cairo in only a few seconds.

Considering the risks involved, we are encouraged to raise awareness about cyber security. Teach children about security so that they grow up fully aware of the risks that surround them. Kids might not necessarily give out your credit card information, but they could innocently open the door for criminals to enter into your network.

The weak password syndrome is something that affects a lot of people. Convenience breeds compromise. You choose a convenient password that you can remember, even if you wake up in the middle of the night and have to blurt it out to save your life. You use the same password on all your devices, online accounts, and networks to make work easier. These are all symptoms of weak password syndrome, and you should try to cure yourself of it. Why?

Because if someone has that password, all of your accounts will become compromised.

Smarter Hackers

One of the biggest challenges for individuals, businesses, governments, and organizations at the moment is that hackers are getting smarter and bolder at the game (Guo, 2016). They directly target entities. In the past, hackers would use bots or weaker attacks to compromise systems, and these only worked when the links shared by the hackers were opened.

Today, we have security protocols in place that render some of these techniques useless. However, hackers have not been resting on their laurels. They have been working just as hard as security companies have been to protect you. Case in point, SamSam is a group of hackers that breached user hard drives, demanding payment to return the information back to the users. They raked in a lot of money in the process.

Most hackers who obtain personal information trade it on the dark web. Once your data is traded, especially if the buyer or the hacker manages to encrypt it, you become vulnerable to any possible attack. You are a sitting duck at that point.

The threat landscape also keeps evolving and growing with time. The game is changing so much that weaker or less-skilled hackers can no longer compete. To survive, the hackers must also step up their game. The problem with this is that, with time, we might end up with organized cybercrime, where only the smartest and strongest criminals can survive. If you've watched enough movies about gang-related crime and territorial disputes, imagine what it would look like if the gangs moved online, being sophisticated and serious about controlling the internet - and the world as we know it.

Expanding the Internet of Things

The internet of things (IoT) is a projection of internet connectivity to our daily lives (Iagolnitzer, Krzanik, & Susini, 2013). It is about moving the internet from the confines of computers and smartphones into everyday activities and services. The supported devices are linked through internet connectivity, electronics, sensors, and other forms of hardware, allowing them to interact with each other and communicate over the internet. These devices can be controlled and monitored remotely.

From consumer applications to smart homes, IoT devices are amazing. You have a system at home that you can activate remotely to change the heating conditions, brightness, turn the lights on or off when you're not at home, and so on.

Given that the IoT space keeps evolving and expanding over time, there is so much more that we are yet to experience. A lot of projects are still in the development phase in their respective labs. As much as the IoT offers an amazing perspective of the future, there are serious risks that must be addressed.

The new fancy systems and devices might be amazing, but they also can be immensely harmful if they're compromised. When compromised, even the most secured networks can be at risk if these devices are connected to them. The following issues are some of the challenges IoT currently experiences:

- **Weak passwords** - One of the risks that users experience with IoT components is easy-to-guess, weak, or hard coded passwords. Once someone has access to these, they can easily take control. Some of the components are built with credentials that cannot be changed.

- **Unsecured network access** - Some of these devices are connected to the internet, yet there is no need for them to be. This presents a challenge, especially in terms of the authenticity, integrity, and confidentiality of the data this device has access to.

- **Inappropriate update protocols** - In the earlier stages, updating most of the IoT devices is not easy. Users aren't aware of when or how to update their systems. Any system that must be updated should have a roll-back feature, just in case the update does not go according to plan. Such features are largely missing.

- **Unsecured interfaces** - Some of the interfaces are not secured properly. From mobile devices to cloud services, the ecosystem can become vulnerable, allowing the hacker access to the device and other components it might be connected to. Hackers no longer need your computer to access your home; they can simply do it by hacking your music system.

- **Default settings** - Many devices are shipped from the production plants to end-users with the default settings. For some of them, users cannot even change the default configurations. This is something that we should not be discussing in 2019. A simple Google search reveals the most basic configuration settings, and these can be used to remotely manipulate the device.

- **No device management** - Some devices do not have security support features, like update management, asset management, response capabilities, and systems monitoring. Some of these devices might be very small and seemingly harmless, but when they are deployed in large numbers, it becomes a challenge. It's like having a wide network of devices that are not properly secured. Once a hacker gains access to one of them, they might as well control all of the others.

- **Data storage and transfer challenges** - Data storage and transfer presents another challenge for these devices. Inappropriate access control measures, lack of encryption protocols, and so on mean that whenever data is accessed through these devices, anyone who is interested can breach and intercept it.

- **Inappropriate privacy protection** - Access to personal information stored in the devices and data that's shared in their ecosystem is very easy. A lot of these devices do not have the necessary protection yet.

- **Outdated components** - Some systems use libraries and software components that can be compromised easily. When breached, the hacker can customize the operating system running the device, making it operate contrary to what it was supposed to do.

Evolution of Hacking Equipment, Tools, and Techniques

Hackers are not the only ones who are advancing; their trade, techniques, tools and equipment are advancing, too. Some of the equipment one may have used to hack into a system a while back are no longer useful.

Hackers consistently build software and hardware that enable them to determine how easily they can penetrate a network. Weak spots in your network are referred to as vulnerabilities. There are so many points on a networked device where vulnerabilities might exist, including the operating system, the browser, and the internet connection.

Some years back, hackers would crash your system. A crashed system immediately becomes redundant. Today, hackers are stealthier. They invade your system without your knowledge and lie in wait. One of the reasons for this is because most hackers today are not generally out to destroy your data or systems but instead just need the data. Data is the new gold. They need to study your systems and collect as much information as possible. Your systems are worth so much more to a hacker when they are up and running efficiently than when they're crashed.

Growing Demand for Data Access

We connect to a lot of devices that need some form of data for us to operate them. Take your smartphone, for instance. After you install an app, you must allow it to access some information about you, such as your location and your messages. Are all these permissions necessary? If you install an app that turns your camera into a flashlight, why does such an app need to know your location? What business does it have reading your messages?

It seems every single application is hungry for your personal data. Most people allow these applications access without thinking twice about it. This data can easily fall into the wrong hands – it almost always does. Given the increasing demand for your data, cyber security is important (Forum, 2012). You must be vigilant about the information you share and the parties you share that information with. Read the terms and conditions of your agreements. You might realize you are signing away your privacy.

Regulations

Cyberattacks threaten the existence of businesses. In the past, businesses were at risk and had to invest heavily in protecting their enterprises and assets. However, in light of the nature of attacks and risk mitigation, regulations like the GDPR have been implemented, which means that organizations must now take as strong of a stand in cyber security as businesses do. They must invest in protecting their digital assets, or they risk heavy fines.

The EU introduced the GDPR as a means of forcing all organizations to go the extra mile in protecting data in their possession. One of the requirements in the GDPR is for organizations to take the necessary measures and implement organizational and technical measures for data protection. They must also review their controls regularly and identify, investigate, and report any breach in their security protocols.

Protecting Yourself from Cyber Attacks

Having seen some of the risks you face, you must take precautionary measures to keep hackers at bay. Some of the recommendations are very simple. You might ignore them altogether, but their effect is far-reaching.

- Always make sure your firewalls are turned on and updated.

- Be careful when downloading files. Most hackers hide malicious code in download files.

- If possible, backup your data to the cloud.

- Never share personal information with anyone who claims they know you or claims to represent a company you interact with. Follow official protocol when dealing with companies and their representatives.

- Ensure your antivirus software and operating systems are updated and upgraded frequently.

- Make sure you visit websites using their official pages and not third party links.

- Make sure you visit a website with an authentic SSL certificate.

- Do not use simple phrases for your passwords, like your date of birth, the names of your loved ones, and so forth.

- Never click on links and emails from sources you are unaware of. This is how phishing is carried out. Hackers do this to steal your personal information.

The cost of cybercrime is steep. You do not want to fall victim or find yourself on the wrong end of the law. You should never take matters lightly when it comes to cyber security.

Chapter 3

Notable Security Breaches

You should be concerned about your security online. Hackers never take a holiday. In fact, at any given time, there is always someone trying to break into some system. Your data is at stake, and we live in a world where demand for data access is at an all-time high. Most of the systems you interact with throughout the day collect some information about you and store it for whatever reasons they present. Most companies collect this data to help them understand you better and scale their products and services to meet your needs.

Data breaches happen every day; almost every hour, there is one taking place. Most of these breaches fly under the radar, because they do not get reported or the victims are unaware they were ever breached. Some companies don't report breaches as they fear such news might negatively affect their financial position in the stock markets.

Over the years, a lot of companies have suffered at the hands of cyber criminals. Considering your interaction with some of the brands mentioned below, you might have also been affected. Given that most companies report cyber security breaches only when they have to, you should always take steps to make sure your data is safe. Precautionary measures include simple things like changing your passwords frequently, using strong passwords, ensuring you sign into online accounts from the official websites, and being keen on the third-party websites and applications that collect additional information from you. Below we have outlined some of the biggest cyber security hacks that rocked the world.

Yahoo

A lot of people currently have email addresses through Gmail, and most people have closed their Yahoo accounts for different reasons. Back in the day, Yahoo was a behemoth - one of the biggest brands in the world. It still is, though its allure has faded over the years. The decline of Yahoo in terms of their control in the email business has been attributed to various things. However, for a lot of people, the breach[5] in 2013 and 2014 was the final straw.

Struggling to remain relevant in the email business, Yahoo was in talks with Verizon to buy the internet giant. More than three billion user accounts were breached. According to Yahoo representatives, they suspect the breach was carried out by a state-sponsored criminal in 2014.

---

[5] Yahoo hack https://www.reuters.com/article/us-yahoo-cyber/yahoo-says-all-three-billion-accounts-hacked-in-2013-data-theft-idUSKCN1C82O1

Some of the information that was breached in this attack includes email addresses, telephone numbers, full names, and birthdates. While people were still coming to terms with this, Yahoo reported later on that in 2013, another group of hackers had illegally accessed at least a billion user accounts. Other than the email addresses, dates of birth, full names and passwords that were not properly protected like those obtained in the 2014 hack, this time around, the hackers obtained security questions and answers that account holders use to protect their accounts or as recovery options when they are unable to sign into their accounts.

How bad were these attacks? Well, the company shed more than $300 million from the sale price. By the time they agreed on the sale, Verizon only ended up paying $4.48 billion for the internet business segment of Yahoo, a company that was once valued at more than $100 billion. Suffice to say, more than 3 billion accounts were affected.

Marriott International

Most people are under the impression that internet access and internet services are the only possible places where security breaches can compromise their information. It is unimaginable to most that a luxury hotel facility like Marriott International could be one of their biggest causes for concern. Well, some half a billion customers of Marriott International[6] had to find out the hard way. This is possibly one of the worst cases of cyber security breaches, given that the hackers had obtained information on customers for more than four years. A Chinese intelligence group whose purpose was to collect credible data on US citizens was blamed for the attack, making this one of the biggest personal data breaches performed by a country.

Marriott International acquired Starwood hotel brands in 2016. However, at the time of the acquisition, the hackers already had a backdoor into Starwood systems from as early as 2014. Even after the acquisition, the hackers still had access and continued obtaining information until they were discovered in 2018.

Some of the victims of this hack only had their contact information and names breached. Other information that was stolen includes guest numbers, passport numbers, contact information, travel information, and a host of other personal information. According to Marriott International representatives, more than 100 million customers had their credit card details compromised, including the card numbers and their expiration dates. However, Marriott International was never certain if the hackers managed to decrypt the credit card numbers.

---

[6] Marriott International Hotel hack
https://www.forbes.com/sites/davidvolodzko/2018/12/04/marriott-breach-exposes-far-more-than-just-data/#12951b4b6297

Home Depot

More than 55 million Home Depot customers had their credit and debit card information stolen from Home Depot in September 2014[7]. From as early as May, the company had suspected their POS systems were infected with malware. Upon further investigation, they realized that the malware in their system was unique and custom-built to be camouflaged as an antivirus program.

In the wake of the breach, Home Depot offered to compensate their US customers around $19.5 million, setting aside $6.5 million for cardholder identity protection services and $13 million to cover their customers' losses.

This settlement catered to more than 40 million people whose payment card data was stolen and at least 50 million others whose email addresses were compromised. The company eventually spent around $161 million on the breach.

JP Morgan Chase

The JP Morgan Chase hack of 2014[8] affected more than 7 million small businesses and 76 million households. JP Morgan Chase is one of the largest banks in the world. The breach that was executed

---

[7] Home Depot breach https://www.forbes.com/sites/katevinton/2014/09/18/with-56-million-cards-compromised-home-depots-breach-is-bigger-than-targets/#72f6e44d3e74

[8] JP Morgan Chase hack https://www.bankinfosecurity.com/chase-breach-affects-76-million-households-a-7395

during the summer of 2014 affected more than a half of all households in the US. Some of the information that was accessed includes email addresses, phone numbers, names, and physical addresses. According to a report that the bank filed with the SEC, some internal information the bank held about their users was also obtained.

According to the bank, none of their customers whose information was accessed lost any money in the process. They also reported that there was no indication that the breach compromised data from the affected accounts.

However, the fact that the hackers had access to root privileges on at least 90 of the bank's servers meant that they had the power to close accounts and transfer funds. The bank reportedly spends at least $250 million each year on security.

Google

Private information about more than 52 million Google+ user accounts were leaked in a three year period between 2015 and 2018. The information included email addresses, names, relationship statuses, job titles, employers, and dates of birth. Following the breach, Google decided to call time on Google+, especially after a *Wall Street Journal* report revealed a software glitch which compromised the profile data for more than half a million Google+ user accounts. In November 2018, Google reported another cyber attack that compromised the accounts of more than 52 million users, and from there, the company decided to end the Google+ project, shutting it down in April 2019.

Uber

Ride hailing app Uber had the personal information of more than half a million drivers and 57 million users breached in 2016[9]. Other than the nature of the attack, Uber was at fault for not handling the breach properly and has since then been used in learning circles as an example of how not to manage such a crisis situation.

Uber learned that two hackers had compromised their system, allowing them access to email addresses, names, and mobile phone numbers for 57 million Uber users. They also obtained driver's license details for more than half a million drivers. To the best of their knowledge, the hackers did not access social security numbers, credit card data, or any other data other than what was mentioned.

The hackers also had access to Uber's GitHub account, through which they were able to retrieve the access credentials to the Uber AWS account. The unfortunate thing is that these are credentials that should have never been on GitHub in the first place.

What irked a lot of people was that it took Uber almost a year to publicly admit the breach had taken place. Other than that, they shot themselves in the foot by paying the hackers $100,000 to destroy

---

[9] Uber cyber attack https://www.theguardian.com/technology/2017/nov/21/uber-data-hack-cyber-attack

any data that they had obtained – without any way of verifying that they had the data or that they destroyed it at all. Uber termed this a bug bounty fee.[10] The company put the blame on their CSO at the time and fired him.

The company's reputation took a massive hit, as did their valuation. By the time of the hack, Uber was in talks with Softbank to sell part of its stake. By the time the sale took place, Uber had shed $20 billion from the initial asking price.

Target

In 2013, more than 100 million Target customers had their contact and credit and debit card information compromised. The hackers targeted the Thanksgiving shopping spree, but the breach was discovered and reported a few weeks later. According to Target representatives, their initial assessment was that the hackers gained access to one of their third party HVAC venders through their POS card readers, collecting information from more than 40 million users. However, a few weeks later, the company reported that personally identifiable information (PII) of at least 70 million[11] customers had been compromised.

---

[10] Uber cyber attack https://money.cnn.com/2017/11/21/technology/uber-hacked-2016/index.html

[11] Target data breach
https://www.forbes.com/sites/maggiemcgrath/2014/01/10/target-data-breach-spilled-info-on-as-many-as-70-million-customers/#750ec781e795

In light of this breach, the company's CIO resigned in March, followed by the CEO in May. The breach reportedly cost the company $162 million. In light of these challenges, the company took measurements to improve their security systems.

Anthem

Anthem is one of the biggest health insurers in the US. In February 2015, hackers stole the personal information of more than 78 million former and current Anthem customers. Through the attack, the names, social security numbers, addresses, employment histories, and dates of birth were stolen from current and former customers. The hackers basically gained access to all the information they would need for identity fraud.

Investigations into the hack eventually concluded that it was sponsored by a foreign government[12] who hired hackers to conduct one of the biggest hacks in the healthcare industry. While the breach was reported in 2015, the execution might have started a year earlier through a phishing email. While the eventual cost of the hack was not disclosed, experts believe it cost the company more than $100 million.

---

[12] Anthem hack http://fortune.com/2017/01/09/anthem-cyber-attack-foreign-government/

Sony – PlayStation

Sony PlayStation was hacked in 2011[13], forcing the company to pull down their services for a month. During this month, the company lost an estimated $171 million due to a hack that compromised more than 77 million accounts. In the gaming realm, this has to go down as one of the worst hacks of all time.

12 million of the 77 million accounts that were compromised did not have encrypted credit card details. Therefore, the hackers had access to users' full names, home addresses, passwords, email addresses, purchase histories, login passwords, and other privileged information. Three years later, Sony agreed to a $15 million settlement in a class action suit in lieu of the breach.

Sony Pictures

Sony was once again in the headlines for all the wrong reasons, this time as victims of a group of hackers going by the name *Guardians of Peace (GOP)*. The hackers leaked confidential data from Sony Pictures[14], which included personal information, employee emails, information about their families, executive salaries, and some of the

---

[13] Sony PlayStation hack
https://www.theguardian.com/technology/2011/apr/26/playstation-network-hackers-data

[14] Sony Pictures hack
https://money.cnn.com/2014/12/09/technology/security/sony-hacking-roundup/index.html

movies that were yet to be released. They further used malware to wipe out Sony's computer infrastructure.

One of the main reasons why GOP attacked Sony was to demand that they do not release *The Interview*, a comedy film whose plot included a plan to assassinate Kim Jong-un, the controversial North Korean leader. The attackers further threatened terror attacks on any cinemas that would screen the film.

Most of the cinemas that had the film in their screening schedules canceled the viewings in light of the terror threats. Sony also canceled the formal premiere and mainstream release of *The Interview*, and instead offered a digital release. According to US intelligence, this hack was sponsored by the North Korean government, considering the network sources, technique, and software employed in the hack. However, the North Korean government has since denied any responsibility for the attack.

This attack led to a back and forth between the two governments, with the US President at the time, Barack Obama, condemning the attack and announcing that the US was within its rights to respond in proportional measures. North Korea was reported to have lost internet access one month from the attack. Russia, on the other hand, appeared to support North Korea, mentioning that it was understandable that North Korea would feel upset about the film. Russia further mentioned that the threats of retaliation by the US were dangerous and counterproductive, given that the US had not provided credible proof of the perpetrators behind the Sony attack.

Adobe

In October 2013, Adobe's systems were hacked, in the process compromising more than 38 million customer records [15]. The company reported that around 3 million encrypted credit card records were stolen, alongside login details for an unknown number of user accounts. Adobe also mentioned that the hackers had access to encrypted passwords and account IDs for around 38 million users.

Following investigations into the hack, it emerged that the source code for some of the Adobe products was also stolen. The hackers also had access to customer IDs, their full names, passwords, and information about their credit and debit cards. In light of this breach, Adobe was made to pay $1.1 million in legal fees, and they also agreed to settle claims to the tune of an undisclosed amount, as a reprieve for the guilty verdict of unfair business practices and for violating the Customer Records Act.

Stuxnet

The main agenda behind the Stuxnet attack was to attack the nuclear power program of Iran. However, other side agendas included disrupting power service grids, public transportation, and the water supply and to present a case for a workable example of worldwide disruption. The attack took place in 2010, but it is reported to have started as early as 2005.

---

[15] Adobe hack https://www.bbc.com/news/technology-24740873

The nature and severity of the Stuxnet attack is one of the reasons why information on it was very scanty, especially in the US. However, experts often consider the Stuxnet worm attack one of the worst, given that it was a cyber breach that had far-reaching and physical effects of an unscalable magnitude.

The US and Israel were behind the Stuxnet malware attack that was meant to target Siemens SCADA systems in the process destroying more than 900 uranium enrichment centrifuges[16]. However, neither of the two countries have ever officially taken credit for the attack.

RSA Security

The RSA Security breach in 2011 was reported to have affected around 40 million employee records. RSA Security is one of the top security companies in the country. The hackers stole SecurID authentication tokens[17]. According to RSA Security, they were victims of two hacker groups that were operating under the protection of a foreign government to target their systems and employees through phishing. In these hacks, the culprits posed as authority figures the employees trusted, while in the process gaining access to the company network.

---

[16] Stuxnet malware https://www.wired.com/2011/07/how-digital-detectives-deciphered-stuxnet/

[17] RSA Security breach
https://money.cnn.com/2011/06/08/technology/securid_hack/index.htm

RSA Security is the security branch of EMC. EMC reported that they have since taken steps to remediate the breach, spending no less than $66 million in the process. They also reported that none of their customers' networks had been affected by the breach.

Experts in the industry, however, believe the company was not being honest about the severity of the attack. In truth, it is no more than a vote of no confidence for one of the top security firms in the country to admit that they were caught unawares. Most people would wonder how they can protect their systems if they are unable to protect their own.

Following the RSA breach, subsequent attacks were meted on other firms, like L3 and Lockheed-Martin, which experts believe were enabled by the success of the RSA breach. The effect of the RSA breach was far-reaching, with a lot of players in the industry suffering psychological damage as a result. RSA is a company that is seen as an icon; they were a role model in the security business, so their vulnerability shocked the entire industry.

Heartland Payment Systems

Hackers used an SQL injection to install spyware into Heartland's data systems. As a result, credit card details of more than 130 million users were exposed. How big was this breach? Think about it. By the time Heartland was breached in 2008, the company was processing around 100 million credit card payments on a monthly basis, for some 175,000 small and mid-size retailers. It was not until January of 2009 that Mastercard and Visa noticed suspicious transactions from some of the accounts Heartland had processed that they notified Heartland of the concern.

As a result of this breach, Heartland was found non-compliant with the Payment Card Industry Data Security Standard (PCIDSS), and until May 2009, they were barred from processing payments for the main credit card providers[18]. Other than that, the company had to settle around $145 million as compensation for fraudulent payments.

The interesting thing about this hack is that the SQL injection vulnerability is something that experts had warned the industry and retailers about for many years, but most of them ignored it altogether. Around that time, SQL injection was one of the most popular attacks worldwide.

eBay

Ecommerce websites are always a hacker's paradise, especially if they find a flaw they can exploit. In 2014[19], eBay fell victim to hackers who stole encrypted passwords, dates of birth, names, and addresses of more than 145 million account holders. The hackers used the credentials of three eBay corporate employees and had unfettered access to the system for more than 200 days. This

---

[18] Heartland Payment Systems hack
https://money.cnn.com/2012/03/30/technology/credit-card-data-breach/index.htm

[19] eBay hack https://www.bbc.com/news/technology-27503290

allowed them sufficient time and resources to access the user database.

In response to the hack, eBay encouraged users to change their passwords. However, they assured customers that financial information like their credit card numbers were not affected, because they were stored in a different database. eBay took their sweet time to report this breach, for which they received a lot of criticism. As a result, eBay experienced a slump in user activity.

US Office of Personnel Management (OPM)

The OPM[20] was targeted between 2012 and 2014 by Chinese hackers who had access to more than 22 million federal employees, including those who were no longer employed by OPM. The hackers had access to the systems in 2012 but were not detected until 2014.

Later on, a different group accessed the OPM in 2014 through a third party contractor, but their actions also flew under the radar until a year later. Some of the information the intruders had access to include personal data, cases with detailed security clearance, and biometric details.

---

[20] US OPM hack https://www.washingtonpost.com/news/federal-eye/wp/2015/07/09/hack-of-security-clearance-system-affected-21-5-million-people-federal-authorities-say/?noredirect=on&utm_term=.0633338ebf44

During an inquiry, former FBI director James Comey mentioned the SF-86 form as one of those whose details were breached. This form is used for employee security clearance and background checks. It contains information about individuals such as the places they have lived, the countries they had visited, their family members, and their addresses.

Equifax

143 million people had their personal information stolen in 2017, including drivers' license numbers, addresses, dates of birth, and social security numbers[21]. Apart from that, credit card information for hundreds of thousands of Equifax customers were also obtained. While Equifax, one of the biggest credit bureaus in the US, reported the breach in July, their representatives believe that the breach may have started earlier in May that year.

Adult Friend Finder

Imagine signing into your favorite casual hookup website, hoping to find someone to satisfy your carnal desires. Most people, afraid that their details might be compromised and accessed by their loved ones or anyone else who uses their devices, try to sign into their accounts from a different browser than the one they often use, perhaps changing their browser to Incognito mode if the browser allows. However, this was never enough for the Friend Finder

---

21 Equifax hack https://www.nytimes.com/2017/09/07/business/equifax-cyberattack.html

Network. Their empire, which includes Adult Friend Finder, Cams.com, Stripshow.com, Penthouse.com, and iCams.com, were breached in 2016[22].

The hackers obtained information from their systems - data that had been collected for more than 18 years in their databases. More than 400 million accounts were compromised, including passwords, email addresses, and full names of the account holders. The Friend Finder Network secured most passwords with a weak SHA-1 hashing algorithm. As a result, by the time this breach was reported, at least 99 percent of the credentials had been decrypted.

VeriSign

One of the worst issues that went along with the VeriSign attack[23] was not the fact that hackers had access to lots of privileged information and systems, but the way the company handled it. VeriSign did not come out publicly to admit they had been hacked until a year following the attack, which was performed throughout 2010; VeriSign only admitted it in line with a new SEC mandate.

The company has never fully reported on the type of information that was stolen or on the impact that it might have on its customers and its business.

---

[22] Adult Friend Finder hack
https://www.theguardian.com/technology/2016/nov/14/adult-friend-finder-and-penthouse-hacked-in-largest-personal-data-breach-on-record

[23] VeriSign hack https://www.wired.com/2012/02/verisign-hacked-in-2010/

TJX Companies Inc.

In December 2006[24], customer information for TJX Companies, Inc. was breached. The information for more than 40 million credit cards was accessed. There are various accounts regarding how this breach was executed. It is alleged that the hackers exploited TJX's weak encryption protocols in the course of a wireless transfer between two of the company's stores, stealing credit card information in the process. There is also another claim that the hackers broke into the network through in-store kiosks that allowed users to apply for TJX jobs.

This hack was orchestrated by Albert Gonzales, the same fellow indicted for the Heartland Payment Systems breach. At the time of this breach, Gonzalez was also working as a paid informant for the US Secret Service. During his sentencing, a government memo reported that insurers, companies, and banks that were affected had lost almost $200 million from this attack.

Cambridge Analytica

More than 87 million[25] people were affected as a result of a Cambridge Analytica data breach in 2015. In this breach, data on

---

[24] TJX Inc. hack
https://money.cnn.com/2008/08/05/news/companies/card_fraud/?postversion=2008080604

[25] Cambridge Analytica scandal
https://www.nytimes.com/2018/04/04/technology/mark-zuckerberg-testify-congress.html

Facebook profiles was illegally accessed, including users' preferences and interests.

A professor from the University of Cambridge created *thisisyourdigitallife*, a personality prediction app which would later share user information to third parties like Cambridge Analytica. Cambridge Analytica is the same company that was running the Donald Trump campaign by creating targeted ads through this data. The company also ran campaign ads in many other countries, including Kenya.

While only around 270,000 Facebook users had installed the personality prediction app on their devices, the data sharing policies applicable in Facebook at that time allowed the app to collect information from their devices and also from their friends.

Facebook

The Cambridge Analytica fiasco may have given Facebook bad publicity, especially since the founder had to go before Congress to defend his company's position. However, the social media giant was not out of the woods yet. Another data breach[26] affected more than 50 million users, compromising personal information like location, relationship status, and contact information. Other data

---

[26] Facebook accounts hacked
https://money.cnn.com/2018/09/28/technology/facebook-breach-50-million/index.html

accessed included the type of devices they used to access their accounts and their recent search history.

During the attacks, which happened in July 2017 and September 2018, the hackers exploited vulnerable codes in the Facebook systems, allowing them access to digital keys through which they could obtain all this information.

Chapter 4

Data Encryption

Data encryption is the process where data is translated into a different code or form, such that the only people who can access and read it are those who have a decryption key, which is also referred to as a secret key. Encrypted data is also known as ciphertext. Unencrypted data is referred to as plaintext. Considering the security threats in the global environment, encryption is one of the best policies businesses, organizations, governments, and individuals are using to protect their data.

Cryptography in Information Security

Information is one of the most valuable assets in any organization. Efforts towards system protection are geared towards three results: confidentiality, integrity, and availability of data. However much someone might try to make you believe it, no security control is 100 percent effective. Encryption is the last prevention mechanism that is often implemented, especially in a layered security model.

Most people hear the mention of encryption and believe they are safe already. This is another fallacy. Encryption is not the end of your troubles. Some hackers have access to very powerful computers that can decrypt any such information. Therefore, encryption is one of many procedures that you can implement to protect your interests.

Cryptography is a scientific concept where complex logic and mathematical equations are used to generate robust encryption methods. Once the meaning of the undersigned data is obfuscated, the artistic element of cryptography comes into play.

Cryptography can be traced back to Sun Tzu's art of war. Field commanders, secret agents and other relevant parties relied on information. To keep this information from falling into the wrong hands, they had to hide its meaning. This allowed them the benefit of surprise, timing, and concealed maneuver. The earliest forms of cryptography relied on codes, transposition, and substitution to conceal their messages.

The threat of cybercrime is always rising. In response, security systems must be built more sophisticated than they were before. Experts keep trying to tighten their grip on communication security in order to make sure there are no loopholes that hackers can exploit. This is done through data encryption. There are two types of data encryption: asymmetric encryption and symmetric encryption.

Asymmetric Encryption

Asymmetric encryption uses private and public keys. Both of these keys are mathematical and perform a specific role within the operation. Data that is encrypted with a public key can only be decrypted with a private key and vice versa; it is impossible to encrypt and decrypt data with the same key.

Private keys must be kept private, lest the security of the entire system is compromised. In the case that you believe the private key has been hacked or compromised in any way, you are required to generate a new one. Asymmetric encryption is considered a stronger and better option compared to symmetric encryption in terms of data protection. However, the challenge with asymmetric encryption is that it's slower than symmetric encryption. As a result, it is not the best option for bulk encryption.

In asymmetric encryption, data is transferred between two parties. Both the sender and the recipient will receive an access key set. The sender must encrypt the information with their private key before it is sent. The recipient on the other hand must use their public key to decrypt the information.

In order to efficiently use this encryption method, digital certificates are used in the client-server communication platform. This certificate holds critical information, such as the location of the user, their email address, the organization to which the certificate originated, the public key of the user, and any other information that can be used to identify the user and their server.

Whenever the server and client need to communicate over encrypted information, they must both send queries across the network, informing the other of their intentions. Once the queries are received, the recipient receives a copy of the certificate. This certificate holds the public key the recipient will need to access the encrypted information.

One of the most prominent uses of asymmetric encryption is in blockchain computing. Bitcoin especially made this form of encryption very popular, because it was used in determining proof of work in Bitcoin mining. In the Bitcoin ecosystem, the Elliptic Curve Digital Signature Algorithm (ECDSA) is used to generate private and public keys. These keys then legitimize the digital transactions involved. Through asymmetric encryption, it is very difficult for anyone to alter any information that has already been loaded onto the blockchain.

Asymmetric encryption is currently being adopted by many businesses and organizations. While it can be scaled up for different purposes, the two main reasons why companies use it are for encryption and creating digital signatures. Digital signatures authenticate data, giving validity to the communications. The recipient is confident that they are accessing information from the sender without the risk of data breach happening anywhere in between. This eliminates the risk of man-in-the-middle attacks.

Digital signatures also confer an element of finality to information shared. The sender cannot claim at a later date that they did not sign or authorize the document. Once their digital signature is appended to it, they are responsible for it.

The commonly used algorithms in asymmetric encryption are:

- RSA
- Diffie-Hellman
- DSA
- El Gamal
- ECC

As soon as the digital signature is verified, the protocol checks to ascertain whether the content is still the same as it was when the sender appended their signature. If any changes have been made to the original copy - even the slightest change - authentication will fail.

Symmetric Encryption

Symmetric encryption is considered one of the conventional encryption methods. It is most likely the easiest. The encryption is performed by using one secret key (symmetric key). Both the recipient and sender have access to the secret key, which is needed to encrypt and decrypt the information. Before the sender dispatches the message, they must encrypt it using the symmetric key. The recipient, on the other hand, must use the same key to decrypt the message.

Considering how simple the encryption and decryption process is, symmetric encryption is easy and takes a shorter time compared to asymmetric encryption. There are many modern approaches to symmetric encryption, which use unique algorithms such as the following:

- **Blowfish** - This is an algorithm that was built to replace DES. It is a symmetric cypher that splits messages into 64-bit blocks and individually encrypts each of the blocks.

- **AES** - This is a standard encryption method used by the US government and a lot of organizations. AES is very reliable in 128 bits but can also be used as 192 bits and 256 bits, especially for resource intensive encryption.

Other algorithms include:

- QUAD

- DES

- 3DES

- RC4

Even without your knowledge, you constantly use symmetric encryption to access the internet. The most common application is when the client interacts with a server that has an SSL certificate. The server and client negotiate a connection and, once approved, they exchange 256-bit session keys to allow communication over an encrypted network.

Comparing Symmetric and Asymmetric Encryption

While asymmetric encryption requires two keys, symmetric encryption only uses a single key. Therefore, symmetric encryption is a rather straightforward approach. Both of these encryption methods access data through a secret key.

While symmetric encryption has been in use for a long time, it does have challenges, especially in secure communication, which necessitates the need for organizations, entities, and individuals to adopt asymmetric encryption. The main advantage that symmetric encryption has over asymmetric encryption is that you can transfer a lot of data through it.

Asymmetric encryption was created in response to the challenge of sharing keys as we see in symmetric encryption. Therefore, with public-private keys, you no longer have to share keys to access encrypted information.

The Role of Data Encryption

There are many reasons why data encryption is an issue you should take seriously. The main reason, however, is to protect the integrity and confidentiality of the data on your computer networks and the transmission over the internet to other computer networks. Modern algorithms are in use today to protect data and replace the data encryption standard (DES), which is an outdated algorithm. Why is encryption important to your business? We have outlined some reasons below.

Protecting data handling - Encryption offers a guarantee of data security all the time. One of the most vulnerable moments in data handling is the point at which it is transferred from one place to another. This is where most hackers pounce. Man-in-the-middle attacks were very common in the past (Li, 2019). A hacker would intercept information, tamper with it, and pass it on to the recipient. The recipient would access and use the data, believing it to be the gospel truth. Through encryption, data is protected when it is in transit or when it is in storage. It does not matter whether you feel the data is important or not, you should always make sure it is encrypted, especially when under storage.

Ensuring integrity - Hackers do not just want to steal your information. Once they have access to it, they can alter it in such a way that it benefits them if someone acts on it as they should have. Unknown to the user, they will be aiding the hacker's objectives. Through encryption, you can ensure the integrity of data is maintained. Skilled hackers can still make a few changes to encrypted data. However, if this happens, the data is corrupted and cannot be used for whatever purpose it was supposed to be used for. Therefore, you immediately realize you have been hacked and initiate the necessary response mechanisms.

The case for privacy - Encryption is important in terms of privacy protection. There is a lot of data that we share with apps, websites and companies. Some companies hold too much data about us;

anyone who has access to it for criminal reasons can execute the perfect identity theft crime. From personal information to location details and credit card information, encryption ensures that this data is inaccessible to the wrong people, especially if they manage to intercept it. They cannot use the data they obtain unless they have the decryption keys.

Encryption, therefore, offers assurance to users that privacy and anonymity online can be a real thing again. Government agencies and criminals can no longer intercept and monitor your communication by doing the bare minimum. The interesting thing about encryption is that some of the protocols and technology available at the moment are too powerful, so some governments are thinking of limiting the effectiveness. This poses risks to individuals, companies, businesses, and other entities. It is almost like locking your door when you leave for work, but leaving the key under the mat.

Compliance - In light of some of the cyber security risks that companies have experienced over the years, several changes have been made, and it is important to comply lest the company is sued for not doing their best to protect the customer data in their care. The GDPR (Smouter, 2018), for example, allows consumers to report any instance where they feel the companies they interact with are not handling their data in a diligent manner.

In most industries, compliance regulations are very strict. The idea here is to make sure that, other than the personal information that the companies hold, their intellectual property rights and any other data that might be privileged is protected from unauthorized access.

One of the regulations the Health Insurance Portability and Accountability Act (HIPAA) demands is that companies must go the extra mile and institute the best security protocols to protect the records of their patients, especially concerning sensitive health information (See, 2003). Encryption is not just about meeting compliance requirements; it is also about protecting the valuable customer data organizations hold.

Cross-device protection - Today, we access the internet and different networks from a variety of devices. All these devices must be protected from unauthorized access. This is where encryption comes in handy. Data transfer is always the riskiest bit of handling data. You might have your company devices protected, but your home devices are not. If you attempt a data transfer on such a device, you risk exposing yourself and the company to unknown dangers. Through encryption, these devices can all be protected, such that you can store and share data across any of the devices you have access to without worrying about someone monitoring your activities or looking forward to intercept your data.

The increasing risk of hacking - Hacking is no longer the activity of a few smart kids who feel bored and have too much time on their hands; hacking is currently one of the biggest businesses in the world. In some cases, hackers operate under the protection of a foreign country. This is just how serious hackers need to get your data. In light of these challenges, encrypting your data makes it difficult for hackers to access it, and even if they do, more often than not there isn't much they can do with it.

Challenges in Implementing Encryption Protocols

Data protection is one of the most common discussions that is being had at the moment. It is a priority that cannot be wished away. Companies that have suffered data breaches in the past also suffered financial losses in terms of compensation packages and expensive lawsuits.

The need for encryption is driven by two factors: compliance and the need to reduce risk. To do this, there exists an elaborate path to encryption that involves classifying risks, discovery, protecting the system, enforcing encryption protocols, and evaluating/monitoring the network to make sure everything runs as it should. Encryption might have been in use for many years, but there are challenges that are unique to the process that must be considered when implementing encryption solutions. We have outlined some of these challenges below.

Performance challenges - Encryption will always add a performance overhead to your systems. The higher your need for encryption, the more you should spend on getting supercomputers that can process large transactions without straining resources. Without this, you must brace yourself for a sluggish performance for all the other systems connected to your network when you are encrypting or decrypting some data.

Managing encryption programs - You have to determine the best encryption method that's suitable for your business. However, this is not the end of your challenges. You must also think about building a plan for system integration and establishing an environment that is secure and reliable.

Are you certain your encryption programs will meet the compliances and requirements in your industry? How easy is it for you to integrate the encryption protocols in data formatting, performance testing, and setting formal policies?

Key length - The other concern that companies experience with encryption is the appropriate key length and algorithms. There are several algorithms available. Choosing the best one depends on the development environment you operate in. At the same time, the ideal encryption key should be longer to reduce the risk of easy decryption. However, at the same time, the longer the key, the heavier network resources you will have to allocate to encryption and decryption. This will definitely affect other parts of the business.

Key management - Key storage and management is the other challenge in encryption. Once you have your data encrypted, where do you store the keys? This is actually a critical discussion. You must consider this in terms of the approaches that are aligned with your business needs. Ensure you keep changing the keys regularly and never use swap keys. Keys must only be accessible on the premise.

Data discovery - How do you access the encrypted data? The business needs swift access to important data. This is a board level decision, from where the relevant stakeholders can agree on the best way and assign data custodians.

Data querying - Querying encrypted data will help with retrieval when needed. This data can be stored on the cloud or on the premise. The challenge for most organizations is that some data will be decrypted several times, especially if it is important to the daily operations of the business. This also increases the risk that hackers might intercept the decrypted data. Remember that subsequent decryption also increases the resource demands.

Encryption Mistakes That Leave You Exposed

Encryption is the subject of many discussions about cyber security today. It has helped to keep hackers at bay, but that is not the end of it. There are a few mistakes that people make that will eventually render their encryption processes useless in the face of attacks.

Think about it - if all these encryption protocols are so good, why is it that governments and businesses are constantly attacked and have loads of data stolen? Over recent years, there are many applications that have made their way into our devices. These applications demand more cryptographic procedures to protect them and support their functionalities. One problem that these applications have is that those who use them do not use encryption protocols the way they should. As a result, the user and the applications end up with a false notion of security, which only becomes apparent the moment they are hacked. We have detailed some of the common mistakes that threaten to derail the success of encryption below.

Using low-level encryption - People are not taking encryption seriously at all. Companies are still encrypting data through file encryption or disk encryption, which are some of the lowest level encryption protocols. Did you know that disk encryption only works when your server is off? As long as your server is on, your operating system will keep decrypting your data such that anyone who has access to the network has access to the data. If there were to be a simple data breach, all of your information will be vulnerable.

Assuming you have the best security experts - One of the biggest mistakes you can make is to assume that the developers in your company are the best security experts in the industry. Your engineers might be some of the most amazing coders you will come across in your entire lifetime, but this does not make them the best in security.

It is sad, but even some of the most brilliant developers in the world come nowhere close to being the best at IT security. IT is a very wide field. It is almost impossible for one person to be experts at all aspects of IT. At the beginning of their careers, most people make the mistake of thinking they can handle anything that is thrown their way. However, once they settle into their careers, they pick a path and specialize in it.

In most cases, security experts are system administrators. Unless their job description says otherwise, you will hardly ever find them writing code. An exception is when you need them to break into some system. One of the challenges that software developers have is pride. They take pride in figuring things out and coming up with solutions to problems. It is, therefore, highly unlikely that any of them will admit that they do not know how to protect your system. In fact, most of them feel threatened and overlooked when you bring in an expert to handle the security of your system. They might even rebel.

Do not find yourself in that trap. Leave security to experts. For encryption implementation, you only have one chance, and you must get it right. If your developer makes a mistake with the code they write, you might notice an error with rendering on a specific web page. However, if this mistake is experienced in security, your entire network might be at risk. To make matters worse, you might not even realize the error in their code until it is too late.

Wrong use of algorithms and cipher modes - When encrypting personal and sensitive data, there are so many algorithms that you can use. Unfortunately, not all of them are suitable for the reasons that you use them. You must do your research to ensure the encryption algorithms applied are suitable. A lot of developers barely understand the risks they put their businesses through with such challenges.

Human interference - No matter how good encryption is, it is useless without the human interface. The weakest link is always the end user. While encryptions might be mathematically sound, their complexity can make it difficult for users to understand and implement them. As a result, some people end up disabling encryption altogether without reporting it to the necessary authorities within the organization. By the time you realize your data was never encrypted, hackers will have already done quite a number on you.

Inappropriate key management - How are you managing the encryption keys? Inappropriate management is the simplest and easiest way for your data to end up in the wrong hands. Even if you use the best encryption program, once you are careless about key management, all your efforts will be futile.

There are so many mistakes people make with encryption keys. Assuming all the information is signed and encrypted properly, some common mistakes people make include keeping the key in a configuration file within the application and storing it on the file system or somewhere within the database.

Some developers do not even protect the keys. They might find a good place to keep the keys, but still leave it vulnerable. Your encryption key is needed to decrypt information, and you should also encrypt the encryption key. This is a procedure referred to as key encryption key (KEK). The KEK should be kept in a different location from your system. It is also possible to protect the KEK with a master signing key or master encryption key. All these are important layers of protection that you should consider, but most people never do.

So, let's say you generate an encryption key that you feel is perfect for protecting your information; however, you use the same key for everything. This is no different from having 123456 as your password. If someone breaks into your system and accesses your encryption key, you can be sure they will try to use it to decrypt anything else that they come across. This lucky guess might be your downfall.

The other challenge is developers who do not plan to change the encryption key. From time to time, you must review your security apparatus and change the encryption keys. The same risk that applies when you use the same encryption key for all services applies here too. Someone will try their luck, and once they are inside your system, they can operate covertly until they achieve their mission.

Regulatory compliance does not guarantee security - The demand for compliance should not be mistaken as a security guarantee. Your networks and systems might be complaint with certain regulations, but this should not mean you lower your guard. While regulations demand that you comply to set standards, some of them barely mention how you should go about it.

In light of this challenge, it is very easy to mess up data security. Unfortunately, when things get rough, the regulations will not cover you. In fact, they will be used to crucify you. To make matters worse, a lot of developers these days add the most basic level of encryption to their code and assume that everything is perfect. This gives your business a false sense of assurance and security, until you realize later on that you were never protected in the first place.

Trusting cloud service providers - Cloud service providers are just like any other business people; they will use beautiful language to interest you in their services. The subscription business is worth billions if not trillions of dollars a year. Given that server-side applications and cloud computing are experiencing an unprecedented growth at the moment, everyone is excited about migrating their businesses to cloud storage platforms operated by giants like Google, Microsoft, and Amazon.

Sure, these service providers take the necessary precautionary measures to keep their services safe. They invest millions of dollars in cyber security to protect their customers and to position their businesses as the best cloud solutions. As a result of this, many people assume that once they create an account and transfer data to the cloud, they are safe, but this is wrong.

While the physical infrastructure that serves these cloud services might be safe, and in some cases, may even offer encryption services, you must perform your own encryption services from your end. Before you move any data to the cloud, make sure it is encrypted. To be fair, data encryption is your prerogative, not the cloud service provider's. In case they offer encryption services alongside the cloud services that you are paying for, this is good for you, because you will enjoy multiple levels of encryption. If they do not, you must ensure your data is protected. Remember that ignorance is never a suitable defense.

While this discussion might paint an ugly picture of the encryption landscape, it is not all doom and gloom. There is a lot that you can do to make sure you are protected, safe, and using the right procedures to protect your data. Consult experts whenever you can.

Debunking Myths About Data Encryption

You do not need to be a cryptographic nerd to understand the concept of encryption or why it is important. It is simple, really; it is hiding your information behind code so that it is useless to anyone who accesses it without the right decryption codes. Over the years, there have been misconceptions that exist about encryption. Most of these are founded on lies or half-truths. The following is a brief assessment of these myths and logical reasons why they are not true.

Encryption Is the Preserve of Big Organizations

One of the biggest misconceptions is this one. Perhaps the origin might be traced back to the fact that, whenever encryption is discussed, the discussions center around big organizations. It is fairly easy to understand why people might think about this.

Encryption is not just for big organizations; anyone who shares information across the internet needs encryption. Today, it is not just the big organizations that are targeted by hackers, but also individuals. No one is safe. As long as you are online, know that someone is always watching.

Did you know that more than 40 percent of cyber attacks target small businesses and individuals? The reason for this is because they are notorious for having weak security systems. Therefore, the cybercriminals can easily find whatever they need from them. Without encryption, someone can hack into your devices and use them as a means of getting into another system. Your devices can be hacked on your unsecured home network, and when you connect your devices to the home network, the hacker migrates to the work network, which was their intention all along.

To prevent your data from falling into the wrong hands, try to make sure you encrypt your data. There are several ways to go about it. You can find simpler solutions for your home devices and appliances. Remember that whether you are running a small business or simply have a personal network at home, encrypting your data is important.

Bogs Down the Network

The issue of encryption and resource consumption is a fair one. Most of the time, you will suffer some sluggish performance on the network when encrypting or decrypting some data. However, you should refrain from using this as an excuse not to encrypt and protect your data. The benefits of encrypting your information outweigh the challenges involved in a slow network performance for the brief duration of time when you are encrypting or decrypting data.

Nowadays, this argument barely holds. We have devices that are built to perform at very high speeds. These devices can handle encryptions without much interference to the network. You might never even notice the network lagging. This is because processors have improved dramatically over the years. You can do so much with very little power in modern times.

Most of the processors we use for computers today are built using AES NI technology. AES NI technology empowers the machines with superior speeds, allowing you to decrypt and encrypt data without a hitch. This technology is reported to enable encryption at three times the usual rate, while it also speeds up the speed of decryption up to ten times.

Implementation Challenges

Implementing encryption is not as difficult as some people imagine it to be. In fact, the most basic form of encryption, SSL certificates, which allow you to browse the internet, actually operate without your knowledge. SSL certificates ensure that the data you access online is protected as you exchange data packets between the browser and your device.

A lot of people still have the notion that you need an expert to install an SSL certificate in your server. This is one of the biggest fallacies as far as encryption is concerned. SSL providers have very simple instructions that you can follow to encrypt your server in a few clicks.

Encryption Is Very Expensive

The issue of affordability is another one that comes down to relative measure. What is expensive for one person might be a drop in the ocean for another. In terms of encryption, a lot of businesses make the wrong assumption that encryption is not affordable, yet you can always enjoy amazing discount offers from different encryption services.

Each encryption program is designed with specific target audiences in mind. Indeed, some of them might be out of reach for you, but not all of them are. You should do some research to find one that meets your needs. This also allows you to test different experiences, and perhaps as you appreciate the services you receive, you might soon see the need to pay more to access the best encryption services in the future.

Encryption Bulletproofs Your System

While encryption will make it nearly impossible for someone to interpret your information, it does not mean you are entirely safe. Theoretically, cracking cryptographic keys might be difficult, but it's certainly not impossible. There are labs around the world that have dedicated their time and resources to find a way around encryption protocols.

Security breaches still happen, even with some of the best encryption procedures in place. One of the reasons behind this is not that hackers managed to decrypt information, but there is poor handling of encryption keys. Some people store their encryption keys in the same systems that they encrypt. You must exercise due diligence when dealing with encryption keys and protocols so that everything you work on is protected.

Encryption Is for Compliant Organizations

It is amazing the lengths to which people will go to avoid encrypting their data, yet it is their resources that are on the line. Of course, any entity that operates in a regulated market must follow the set guidelines, or they will lose their license to operate. Data security is serious, and authorities are taking a firm stand on it. Companies must exercise due diligence to protect their customers.

Whether you are obligated to encrypt your data or not, it is a logical concept to encrypt sensitive data, as it may fall into the wrong hands, resulting in you fighting legal battles that might run your company into the ground.

The SSL Encryption Myth

SSL is an encryption method that protects your data when browsing online. Given that it almost always just works without any input from your end, many people assume that it encrypts all the data. This is not true. SSL only encrypts data that is being transferred. It does not protect static data. You should take the initiative and encrypt all the data you have access to, especially since it is written on the disk.

Encrypted Data Cannot Be Stolen

You must realize that there is no security program or project that can offer you 100 percent protection, as mentioned earlier. The best security products in the market will try to offer the top protection to the best of their knowledge. However, a lot of factors come into play that migcouldht make it difficult for these programs to protect your data accordingly.

The safest companies and individuals are those who believe that their data is never safe, and as a result, they keep looking for ways of protecting their data. If you believe your data is protected by virtue of the fact that you encrypted it, you become a sitting duck and might only realize your mistake once your data is wiped clean or the FBI is at your doorstep, accusing you of a crime you have no idea about.

Chapter 5

Initiating Breach Protocol

So, let's say the worst case scenario happens. You wake up one day preparing for work but your phone cannot stop ringing. Notifications keep dropping in like raindrops. You resist the temptation to check your phone until you get to the office. By now, you are probably certain something big is happening, and the anxiety is killing you. When you get to the office, it is chaotic. Everyone seems to be busy with something, people are running around, and you notice most of your superiors are holed up in meetings you were never aware of. Then it hits you - you've been hacked.

This is one of those scenarios everyone dreads, but at some point in the modern digital sphere, you must prepare for it. If you are lucky, you might never have to deal with it. The most important question: do you have a breach protocol?

There are different ways of dealing with a breach. The first few hours from the moment you notice you have been compromised are important and will determine how you make it out of this situation.

Dealing with a hack is no different from dealing with a terrorist attack. Hackers are terrorists. Think about the 9/11 attacks. After the first attack, rescue operations were mobilized to manage the situation. However, a second blast followed that compounded the loss, given that members of the rescue team were soon added to the list of victims.

You need an elaborate breach protocol in the event of an attack. Without one, you might rush into the scenario, triggering an avalanche of events that would effectively see you complete the hacker's mission. Some hackers invade your system hoping for total annihilation. They execute a hack so perfect, a chaotic response in the wake of unearthing their activities in your system could end up being just as catastrophic.

Assembling a Task Force

No matter what is happening or what is at stake, one thing is certain - you have been hacked. Your nakedness is exposed for the whole world to see. The last thing you want to do is go into panic mode. To manage the situation, you must think clearly and swiftly. Resist the urge to shift blame or point fingers. At that point, the entire company is under attack, so no one really cares about the department responsible for the vulnerability exploits. Your company's brand is probably trending on social media by that time with news networks carrying breaking news stories about your company.

Hacks happen, but it is not the end of the world. You must have a plan in place to enable your team to focus on what lies ahead. The pressure will be intense, but everyone must follow the set protocol. Depending on the size of your organization and the resources at your disposal, you might need a crisis management team.

Call an emergency meeting and inform all the employees of the current status. Remind them that during this turbulent time, they must stay calm, and if possible, avoid social media. They should not respond to or discuss anything about the hack with anyone. All matters concerning the hack will be responded to by someone specifically appointed by the company to deal with this particular issue.

Hold discussions with the relevant department heads, and try to understand the situation as soon as possible. Also, identify technical flaws in your system that might be responsible for the hack, and ensure you have someone ready to deal with the media and handle customer communication and relations appropriately.

Remember that your customers are trying to understand what is happening just as much as you are trying to understand the situation. If you do not address their concerns in a timely manner, the situation might spiral out of control very fast. There is always the risk that you might be looking at litigation in light of the hack, so be certain to have a legal team ready to start investigating and looking at the possible solutions. This is not the time to be caught unawares.

One of the mistakes that most companies have made in the past is to stay quiet about hacks, only revealing the truth after they are pressured into action by authoritative parties. If you do this, your customers will feel cheated, and you'll then have a bigger issue to deal with. In case your business is not so elaborate to have all these protocols in place, get in touch with a relevant third party as soon as you realize you are compromised, and have them guide you on how to proceed.

Containing the Situation

The taskforce that responds to a hacking incident might serve different roles depending on the nature of the attack. While you handle the PR nightmare that follows, you should have people working behind the scenes to contain the damage. One of the first things they must do after identifying the problem is think of a solution to patch it. Patches will offer a temporary fix to your technological challenges or eliminate the virus that might have crippled your systems.

A good example of this is the Heartbleed bug from 2014 (Gujrathi, 2014; Sanchez, 2014). At least 17 percent of servers on the internet were affected. As soon as the bug was detected, a security patch was available almost instantaneously. Those who were quick to respond arrested the problem before it got out of hand. Some network administrators, however, were too slow to respond, and as a result, their servers were left exposed longer than they should have been.

You will almost always need to reset your passwords in the aftermath of a security breach. You might not be aware of how much data was compromised or the nature of data that was compromised, so to be safe, it makes sense to encourage everyone to change their passwords.

Pull devices off the internet and institute a quarantine for any devices that were exposed or might have been exposed. If the hack was an inside job or assisted by someone with insider access, block their accounts, revoke their access, and have your security team investigate their devices to understand their role in the hack and how deep it runs. Take all necessary steps to make sure that the attack does not compromise the integrity of your organization or any investigations into the matter.

Assessment

Who was affected? How much data did you lose? What is the nature of data that was lost? What steps should you take in light of the data compromised? You might not be able to determine the nature of compromise immediately. Therefore, you must be careful and conservative concerning the way you proceed. You can also bring in an expert to help you understand the extent of the attack and to advise you on the necessary cause of action.

Having understood the compromised data, find out how this data can be used in the hands of the attackers. A severe breach is one where the stolen data can be used for criminal acts such as identity theft. You must escalate this to the relevant authorities as soon as possible. If your data was encrypted, the risk is relatively lower, but depending on the type of encryption, you still need to be vigilant.

Your response to the hack also depends on the context. Was it a targeted hack or a general breach in security? A targeted hack implies that the attackers were looking for something specific, and if they found it, your problems might be greater than you suspect them to be.

Mitigating Future Attacks

An attack presents you with a peculiar chance to reassess your security position and improve your systems. You can look back at the lessons learned from the attack and bolster your defense mechanisms. Speak to a security consultant and get a professional perspective on your current security protocols. This is a good way of making sure you never suffer the same risk again.

Address the security flaws that were exposed in the hack, and make the necessary changes, documenting them accordingly; this documentation will be useful for future references. Train your personnel regarding any changes you make to strengthen your security processes so that they are aware of what is expected of them. Any arrangements or agreements you had with service providers should be reviewed to make sure that they conform with your present changes and meet the necessary security obligations.

Management has the necessary tools and oversight capabilities to deal with a breach when it happens. There is so much data available at their disposal that can be used to understand the reasons behind a cyberattack and how to prevent one in the future.

Each attacker has a different mission. The nature of business systems is also unique to every situation and industry. Therefore, the same response mechanisms will not apply to everyone. You must review data from different sources to help you prescribe the right response mechanisms for your predicament. The recommendations below can be considered depending on their feasibility and applicability to your organization's position.

Understanding your risk profile - Companies, individuals, and businesses are exposed to different risks depending on the niche they operate in. By understanding the nature of your business environment, you have a better shot at determining the possible risks you need protection against. Of course, there might be a few scenarios where some risks catch you off guard, but a careful analysis should help you prepare for risks that are inherent to the nature of your business or the industry environment.

In a highly competitive industry, for example, you will almost always have to worry about your competitors spying on your research and development processes to get an edge above you in the market. Once you understand the risks you are up against, it is easier to institute appropriate cyber security procedures and incentives.

Executive support - Most organizations with the best security systems enjoy support from top level management. Without their goodwill, it is almost impossible to implement the right security systems, practices, and protocols. It is mandatory in the digital age that companies are run by management teams that understand the important role that security plays. Security should always be a part of the organization's cultural practices.

Screening employees - Businesses depend on employees to handle confidential data with diligence. However, not all employees share the same goals and moral ethics as the stakeholders and business owners. Some people are in the business to earn a living. Others are not aware of what they are doing in their lives, so as long as they are paid to work, they are happy.

Employee screening should not be limited to searching for the appropriate skills to enable employees to work in the company, but should also consider the suitability of employees in terms of their core beliefs, and if these are aligned with the organization's core objectives. Considering that the weakest link in any system is usually the human interface, you must take employee screening seriously to ensure you have people who are working towards the same goals as the business.

Proper training - Get the necessary training to ensure your employees are aware of the policies that man their operations. Compliance is an important part of mitigating security breaches. Given the implementation of the GDPR, you should train your staff to help them protect all data they come across and to avoid the risk of heavy penalties.

Other than general training, individuals who handle highly sensitive information should receive special training to enable them to carry out their mandate without any challenges. These individuals are key to the survival of your company, and in the unlikely event of a breach, they will be the ones who help you start a new chapter.

Addressing threats with the seriousness they deserve - It might sound uncanny, but a lot of businesses barely treat security risks with the seriousness they deserve. While a lot of companies already understand the risks they face in their businesses, most of them do not do anything about it. They ignore and assume that they are not the targets of attackers, assuming that hackers are only after big businesses.

What these business owners fail to realize is that hackers can do so many things with the information they have. Digital signatures can be altered and used in cybercrimes. Hackers can obtain information about you from your networks and devices, information that you might not be aware you had in the first place. Hackers barely go after your system for the sake of just attacking a system; there is always something useful to them in your system. Your data might seem relatively less valuable than data from a large corporation, but you never know what a hacker will do with it.

Keeping updated systems - You would be surprised to learn that many companies do not update their systems, and a vast majority do not even use legitimate software. Many people use cracked and pirated software, which defeats the purpose of privacy and security. A cracked program is one that, by default, already has loopholes in its code. These loopholes are exploited by hackers. Some of the hackers prepare these cracks and release them through torrents and other file sharing platforms where they can be downloaded by the masses.

Most people who use such programs do so because they feel the legitimate versions are too pricey. However, the price they eventually pay for using pirated software is too steep. It is safer to buy the original program and install it. Besides, using pirated software is infringing on the developers' intellectual property rights, and you can be sued for this.

Backups - How often do you backup your data? It is advisable that you have several backups in different places. Currently, many people and businesses backup their systems and data to a cloud storage facility. However, that is not enough. You should also have data backed up in a separate and off-site facility.

Backups enable you to reboot your operations in the aftermath of an attack without many challenges. Without backups, you may never be able to recover from a hack. Never overlook the importance of saving your data elsewhere, especially for data that is critical to the core operations of the business.

Enforcing policies - Policies are only as good as the efforts to enforce them. If you have some good policies but cannot enforce them effectively, they might be useless. Most entities limit their policies to passwords, but passwords are not enough to protect you.

You should go the extra mile and document your policies on security procedures and processes.

When enforcing policies, ensure the executive arm of the business is providing support. People will see the seriousness in policy enforcement when the top management acts in such a manner to suggest that they are working hand in hand with the business towards meeting the core objectives of their operations. While enforcing policies, you must also realize that some members of the workforce are not tech savvy. For this reason, make sure you simplify the policies so that they too can understand what is expected of them.

Investing in security - Invest in security. This is the simplest solution to most of your security concerns. Do not overlook the need for a robust security platform. Make sure you consult industry experts on the risks associated with your operation. From there, discuss a plan of action and how to implement business policies in your organization, supported by the necessary security apparatus.

One thing that you might already be aware of is the fact that there is no one-size-fits-all mechanism in cyber security. Due to this, you should not always be loyal to hardware or software vendors. Make sure you are constantly looking for better and more efficient alternatives.

Chapter 6

Preventing Cyber Attacks

What can you do to prevent cyber attacks? Do you have the right systems and procedures in place to protect your company against an attack? Between 2017 and 2018, many organizations suffered from some form of cyberattack. Most of these were attributed to inappropriate security measures. Some organizations simply did not have a robust security platform in place, so hacking them was basically as easy as hacking into an individual's computer at the local library.

Types of Cyber Attacks

Human behavior is one of the worst enablers for cyber hacks. It is very easy to allow a criminal into your secure platform. All they need is to gain the trust of someone, and you are finished. Therefore, it is important to learn how to identify threats and from there, how to protect yourself from those perceived threats.

There are two broad categories of cyber attacks: semantic attacks and syntactic attacks.

Semantic Attacks

A semantic attack is about social engineering. These attacks are performed by altering someone's behavior within the organization targeted by hackers. The software involved plays a very small role, unlike in syntactic attacks. Semantic attacks are basically about perception (Noor et al., 2017)

Phishing is one of the most popular semantic attacks in which hackers send an email hoping to collect some information from the victim. You might not be aware of the phishing attack until it is too late, because the hackers clone emails from correspondence you interact with regularly. These are people you trust, so you barely crosscheck to make sure the emails are legitimate.

Once you click a link in the email, you are asked to provide some information to help them verify your account. In doing so, you willingly provide all the access credentials hackers need to take you down. Some phishing attacks can also include viruses and worms. However, the modus operandi is to dupe you into believing the email address is legitimate, willingly providing the information hackers need. The worst bit about social engineering is that some attacks are a combination of semantic and syntactic attacks, and as such, the effects can be devastating.

Syntactic Attacks

A syntactic attack comes after your network through different channels. These attacks are often carried out through malicious programs. The most common programs used for syntactic attacks are as detailed below.

Trojan horses - A trojan horse is something that looks harmless. You will allow it into your system, unaware of the danger it possesses. Today, trojan horses can be sent using several methods, including hackers cloning an email. The email will look like it comes from someone you know or trust, but its main purpose is to steal your information or destroy your system - whichever reason the hackers sent it.

Worms - Worms are unique. They do not need the action of another program to spread through your computer or network. Worms are often deployed as secret agents. They collect and report information about your network to the hackers. They spread very fast in a network and can cripple it as soon as the hacker accomplishes their goals.

Viruses - A virus is basically a program that is attached to another program or file. They replicate when you access the infected program or file. Viruses are common in shared and downloaded files and attachments sent through email. When the virus is activated, it can send itself to every person on your contact list.

How to Protect Your Business

You need to implement a good security plan and some strategies that will help you secure your platform and protect your interests. In light of the adoption of the GDPR, a lot of companies are making changes to their operations. (Perhaps the threat of heavy fines might be working after all.) One of the benefits of the GDPR is that it allows the average consumer to take back control over their data and how it can be accessed. With this in mind, customers can also report whenever they feel the company is not doing enough to protect their data. To ensure you do not find yourself on the wrong side of the law, we have included a few guidelines that can help you protect your networks and prevent a cyber attack.

Threat Identification

Make it a habit of reporting any threat to your system. Something as simple as unauthorized access might not mean much to you until it is too late. Nothing is ever too small to report when it comes to cyber security. The subsequent loss of information or denial of access to important services is proof of this.

These days, a lot of companies handle information that is very sensitive. This is information that would attract most hackers, especially when they realize your systems use weak security protocols. Remember that hackers are always trawling the internet looking for vulnerabilities that they can exploit. You should not allow them this opportunity.

If someone is going to hack you, at least make their life difficult while attempting it. Take the appropriate precautionary measures to keep the important information about your company safe. Identify and report threats as soon as they happen so that the relevant parties and authorities can look into them and clear your conscience about them before things get out of hand and you lose everything.

Expect an Attack

In the digital world today, it is prudent to expect that an attack is always imminent. This way, you will go about your operations expecting an attack at any given time. With this in mind, the business operations will be carried out with all checks and balances in place.

Try to determine the kind of information you handle and classify those that might be extremely important to hackers from those that are not. Hackers might come after your company for any kind of information. Some might camp in your systems hoping to find a leeway into another company's systems, especially if you deal with other large corporations as third parties.

Astute risk assessment processes will help you make sure you have the right solutions for your problems as soon as they arise. You might not be sure about the type of information you handle, which might be alluring for hackers, so the best way is to make sure everything is protected.

Employee Management

No one has the best insight into your business like your employees do. They are the people who keep your business running and alive. It is only fair that you keep them happy and motivated to work towards the same goals your business has.

In the digital era, loyalty is hard to come by. Your desire to have employees who will do all they can to protect the sanctity of your organization might not be achievable. However, you can take steps to ensure that you never have to risk being shot in the foot by the people you trust. A motivated workforce is always a good thing.

Other than motivating the employees, try to ensure they are aware of their roles in the organization and about the data protection that's required by law. Ensure everyone understands their responsibility and the limit of their liability for the data they handle or protect. Some people freely give away information at times inadvertently, because they are not aware of the risks involved or of the legal ramifications of their actions. Properly educating employees on their legal responsibilities can save you in the long run.

Try to foster an environment where people take responsibility for their actions. This encourages employees to be honest and realize that they're in control of something. They are caregivers and protectors of something important. That being said, you must also take precautionary measures by installing an additional layer of security beyond what you expect employees to do on their part. Your employees might not always be working towards the same goals as you. Where possible, use a password manager to make sure everyone is using an appropriate password.

Two-Factor Authentication

Everyone is using it, so why not implement it for your company? You may have noticed that most of the applications you use have switched to two-factor authentication. From Facebook to Gmail, everyone is adding an extra layer of protection for your data. Try to do the same for your company.

Two-factor authentication helps to secure your systems and data by adding an additional verification step to access accounts. Encourage all your employees to use it. Once you enter the password, you receive a message on your phone, without which you cannot access the accounts. This makes it difficult for attackers to go after your system, forcing them to find an alternate way to do so.

While you might not be able to stop hackers from trying to attack your systems, you can do your best to dissuade them altogether. Making the access process as inconvenient and difficult as possible is one of the best ways of achieving this.

System Audits

When was the last time you conducted a system audit on your network? Are you certain about the health status of your network? You need an in-house audit and an external audit to make sure your system is not compromised.

Via a thorough audit, you can learn so much about your vulnerabilities you are exposed to. An external system auditor will also advise you on your current state of affairs in light of industry regulations, so that you can improve your systems and operate a compliant business.

When you start your company as a small firm, things like system audits barely make sense to you, and it seems like you're just spending money that you don't have. You might even consider it once in a very long time. However, as the business grows, you will get a the point where the need for a system audit becomes mandatory. An audit helps you reduce the risks of being hacked. There are so many experts in the industry who can assist you with a system audit, including people who have been in the cyber security industry for many years. Their understanding of cyber security will work to your advantage and help you protect your business.

Signing Off Policies

If you issue mobile devices, tablets, and laptops to your employees, ensure they sign them off before they leave the company. This is important so that privileged information is not leaked. You must also look into encryption protocols for any information that is passed through your networks and devices. The idea here is to maintain confidentiality and integrity.

Insurance Policy

It is prudent in this digital age to have insurance against cyberattacks. Hackers are all over the place, and considering the nature of data and information you process, it's strongly advised that you find an insurance policy that suits your operation. When discussing the risks involved with your insurer, you can learn a lot about the challenge ahead and take that as an incentive to address the possible risk scenarios. An insurance policy will cover your business in the event of a cyberattack. However, by taking the initiative to improve your security based on the risks discussed, you will save yourself from a lot of unnecessary challenges.

Cyberattack Resilience

The nature of risks you are exposed to once your business is connected to the internet is tremendous. Hackers can have extremely detrimental effects on your operations. A lot of companies today depend on the internet, social networks, and technology to remain competitive in their industries. You need to make sure your company is cyber resilient, so you can avoid risks associated with business downtime, revenue loss, and many other costs you might not be aware of as yet.

The size of your company does not matter. Anyone can be a victim of a cyber attack. Taking preventative measures to protect your business will help you gain an advantage in terms of securing your business by reducing your risk exposure. Besides, an astute security profile will also work in your favor, helping you improve your brand image and business reputation, and it can improve your appeal to investors.

Software Updates

One of the simplest ways of protecting your business from attacks is making sure you use updated software. Tech giant HP revealed that applying a software patch at the right time can prevent at least 85 percent of targeted cyber hacks. Software developers often release patches for their programs as frequently as necessary, and more often in response to prevailing cyber threats in the global business world. With this in mind, make sure you get the latest update of whatever software you are using. Regular updates keep your systems protected from vulnerabilities. That is why developers release updates from time to time.

Penetration Testing

Not all hackers are bad people. Some hackers are good for your business. To ensure you run a technologically healthy and sound business, you should consider hiring an expert to perform penetration testing and assess the vulnerability of your systems. This is something you should do regularly. You can do it monthly, quarterly, or even annually, depending on what works best for you. The results of these tests will help you identify where your weaknesses lie, and the consultant will also advise you on how to deal with them.

The Need for Proper Training

If you have the best and most secure system in the world but your employees are unaware of how to manage it, you serve no purpose. Training is important to protect your businesses. Most employees unknowingly welcome hackers into your world. They lack the basic understanding of security policies and practices, and how to avoid attacks.

Many companies have their employees signing into computers at cyber cafes with their official business accounts, and at the same time, they forget to sign out and erase their browsing history when they're done.

Other than training your employees, you must also remind them frequently about the policies they have learned and how to enforce them. Ensure everyone adheres to the set guidelines or your employees will be your weakest link, as they always are. Alongside training, make sure everyone learns the importance of taking responsibility for their actions. Employees must protect their departments and dockets. Data access is a critical aspect today that should not be taken lightly. Once everyone understands their responsibilities and accountability for devices in their care, you will have an easier time mitigating cyber hacks.

Protect Your Emails

Among other attacks, phishing attacks are mostly propagated through emails. This is an elaborate form of social engineering where the hackers convince the recipient that they are someone they should trust. Considering that emails are the primary form of communication at the moment, there are many risks involved in using unprotected emails. To protect your emails, you should invest in an anti-spam service that screens your company emails.

Virtual Private Network (VPN)

It's advised that you purchase VPN software and ensure all employees install it. If they need to access the company services and they are not within the premises, they must first connect the VPN. VPNs encrypt all information that is exchanged through them, improving your security. With a policy like this, all communication takes place over an encrypted channel. Some organizations even run VPN services at work, making it difficult for anyone to breach their systems.

Disaster Management Plan

Make sure you have a solid disaster management plan in place. In the event of a data breach, you should have a recovery plan that will restore your business to full operation in no time while you try to solve the issues behind the scenes. A disaster management plan is not a one-off thing. The plan must be tested periodically and updated to meet the current business demands and highlight resilience to present cyber attack risks.

Privileged User Access

Everyone at your company cannot have the same level of access. Some people only need limited access to enable them to carry out their operations. This especially applies to data access. Some elements of the data in your possession should be restricted to employees with high privilege access.

In data management, you must make sure you have the right controls so that everyone has unique administrative abilities over the data systems your business runs. Sensitive information should only be accessible to very few people in the business.

Another challenge that you will experience is the proper management of removable media. These are the easiest ways for most cyber threats to breach your system. Someone walks in with a USB drive and plugs it into their work computer, hoping to copy their favorite playlist for work. However, the USB drive is infected, and just like that, their computer also is. The infection will soon spread and before you know it, if this was a targeted attack, your business is under siege.

Insist on scanning removable media before it's used in your network; or alternatively, ban them altogether. Encourage users to share information across networks. Networks have firewalls in place that can prevent the transfer or sharing of compromised files. Today most companies have very fast internet access in their offices. Even at home, most people are connected to reliable internet services. You can share gigabytes of data in a very short time. Instead of copying the file, upload it to a cloud storage facility, and share the link for the user to access it at their own time. This does not just save you from waiting for the file to download, but it also saves you on space.

DDoS Protection

DDoS attacks are often targeted attacks. The hackers program a network of computers to direct excess traffic to your website or business. This flood overpowers your network resources, preventing your users from accessing your services. You might also have to pull down your network while you try to solve the problem. These days, there are several prevention mechanisms you can use to protect your business from DDoS attacks.

Gateway Layer Protection

One of the weakest elements in any network is the access point to which your business is connected to the internet. This is the gateway layer. Most attacks are perpetuated through the gateway layer. A lot of them pass by undetected, and you only realize them when your system is hijacked. Update your security apparatus, and make sure you have antivirus programs that can filter web content and protect the gateway layer.

Personal Devices

Encourage employees to avoid bringing their personal devices to work. Personal devices might not have the same security protection as the official work devices do. Leave them at home, and at the same time, do not sign into company accounts on your personal devices. Depending on the nature of your business, it is advisable to issue specific devices to your employees that they can only use at work.

Additional Protection for Critical Operations

All aspects of your business do not hold the same weight. Some are more important than others. Most security breaches target critical information about your business. These are the bits of information upon which the foundation of your business is built. It is wise to provide a higher level of security for this kind of data. Whatever security you use for every other aspect of your business, you should take it a notch higher for the critical elements. Encrypt your communications and data transfers concerning these operations.

State of the Business Address

Remember how the president gives the state of the nation address, updating audiences about the current state the country is in? You should do the same for your business. You might not need to speak to an audience the size of the president's but make sure you inform the relevant parties of the state of the business. How do you do this?

First, you must make sure you have protocols and procedures in place that will guide your operations and ensure that all employees are aware. Review your operations, possible threats, and improve your protection. Make sure that employees are aware of any intrusion detection methods in place so they are confident in the robust nature of their employer. When employees are fully aware of how secure the system is, they will often be taken aback when they notice something fishy, reporting it immediately. This way, everyone in the system is vigilant.

Conduct a mock drill from time to time to evaluate how resilient your protection is. These drills will also help you understand how your employees respond to crisis situations, and you can use that as a necessity for further training. You want the entire workforce ready and able to contain a breach in the unlikely event that you are attacked. Without this, they might make the situation worse.

Endpoint Protection

One of the biggest challenges most businesses struggle with is protecting endpoint access points - in this case laptops and PCs. These devices are vulnerable to attacks, because the employees are not careful about their personal security. Most employees take security measures for granted. Encourage all employees to protect their devices and keep them updated.

Make Cyber Security Everyone's Prerogative

You cannot protect the company on your own. Securing the fortress should be everyone's job. Work with the relevant parties to institute holistic measures regarding cyber resilience. Ensure everyone is aware of their role in protecting the company and their accountability in lieu of their roles.

One of the easiest ways of doing this is by passing a policy stating that everyone must create a strong password, complete with examples of strong passwords. Other than that, insist that passwords must be changed frequently. Assess your employees, procedures, and processes frequently to make sure that your security protocols are up to date and current in light of the pertinent risks you are exposed to.

Chapter 7

General Data Protection Regulation (GDPR)

What is General Data Protection Regulation (GDPR) about? In 2012, in realization of the EU's laxity in preparedness for the digital age, the European Commission decided to take a stand that would see the region get ready for the internet age. More than four years later, they came to an agreement on GDPR and how it would be enforced.

The GDPR is a framework whose guidelines affect all member states to the EU, including the organizations, individuals, and business, not just in Europe, but beyond. There is not much trust going around on the internet. However, this does not mean it should be ignored and become a new normal. Through the GDPR, the EU realizes that the future of the digital economy can only be structured upon a foundation of trust. The standards of data protection recommended in the GDPR are common and shared across different countries.

The GDPR further seeks to ensure that consumers are empowered and realize that they wield a lot of power in terms of how their information can be accessed and to whom it can be shared. Consumer power in data access and protection has been missing for many years, with a lot of people feeling like they are slaves to whatever rules that apply. Through the GDPR, however, all of this changes.

The rules and regulations outlined in the GDPR allow consumers more power and control over their data, even in the hands of organizations. Compliance with the GDPR is meant to ensure there is a level playing field in terms of data access, both for the businesses and consumers, especially in the digital economy.

Impact of GDPR on Governments

Businesses all over the world are more concerned about their customer data today than they were prior to May 25th, 2018, on which date the GDPR came into effect. However, it is easy to narrow down the impact this regulation has on businesses and overlook one important entity: the government. Governments are also not spared when it comes to consumer privacy.

GDPR is a brilliant idea, not just for businesses and customers, but also for the economy and national security. In the long term, the global economy will be better with the GDPR fully implemented. It is understandable right now that some companies are uneasy about the policies and implementation, but that will pass.

About security, on the face of it, GDPR might appear to be a bad thing for business. Companies whose businesses are run online that don't have the necessary systems in place to meet the GDPR requirements will have to rebuild their business systems from scratch. To remain in compliance, they must also make sure they adapt their business model in general.

When you look at it from this perspective, it almost sounds punitive. Those who cannot comply will be forced to ship out or incur the expensive cost of setting up a new business process. However, there are strong security incentives in this regulation for investing in security. Companies that are proactive will be able to take advantage and set themselves in a prime position to be at the helm of the internet compliance revolution that will happen in the next few years.

Before GDPR, there were very few incentives for companies to consider protecting consumer data. Hacks would appear as the incentive for companies to invest in protecting their businesses to restore the trust their customers and other stakeholders have in their business. What this means is that, without a breach, most companies would keep operating blindly. It was also relatively impossible to determine the real cost of a cyber hack until it happened. In boardroom meetings, stakeholders would probably float speculative figures that they might spend on security, without a certainty that it would offer credible returns.

Narrow this down to governments and the public sector. These speculative sums are obtained from taxes. It is repugnant to throw around figures for a speculative cause without having a solid backing as to why the public sector must spend that much money on a given system.

For the public sector, the important provisions in the GDPR that must be addressed for compliance are outlined below.

Consent for International Data Transfer

The public sector often struggles with consent, especially when data is involved. GDPR allows entities to transfer data. However, the data transfer must be subject to and limited to specific subject areas.

The idea here is to mitigate the relational disparity between citizens and governments. Governments often demand that citizens offer their information freely. After all, all citizens and their livelihoods are property of the state. In the event of a legally binding instrument that is enforceable by law between different government entities, the GDPR allows special privilege for the entities to share data with other countries in the absence of the normal safeguards; this would need to be under dire circumstances.

Request Compliance Status Information

When meeting external suppliers or potential suppliers, it is advisable that you find out about their GDPR compliance. Government bodies are within their mandate to demand to know how these entities manage data in their operations. Data controllers and processors are important people to deal with when doing business with external companies. The role of the data controller is to generate and own data. The data controller, therefore, must offer clear steps on how to protect data in their possession. Data processors, on the other hand, are just people who use data that they are provided by the data controller. Therefore, from this understanding, GDPR encourages government agencies to try to vet their suppliers well before they commit to doing business with them.

Legitimate Interest for Processing Personal Data

Authorities are barred from claiming legitimate interest as a legal defense for their decision to process your personal data. Thus, authorities must henceforth seek alternative legal reasons especially if they had been relying on legitimate interest all along.

They must go back to the drawing board and look at their processing activities to determine whether they can process personal data under a different auspice. In case this is not possible, they are barred from processing personal data.

Create the Position of a Data Protection Officer

Government offices and agencies are now mandated to create the position of a data protection officer. As long as these agencies or offices process some personal data, they must appoint a data protection officer. In the private sector, the conditions are different. The data protection officer is only needed if specific criteria are met in the private sector.

GDPR, however, allows agencies to share a data protection officer between departments and organizations, but only if the resource sharing is credible in light of the size and structure of the entities in question. Local authorities and legislature must also be consulted to determine whether there is a need for further requirements like having the data protection officer registered in the local government register.

GDPR is lauded for the input and interest in protecting personal data within the public sector. The changes to personal data are restricted, which brings about transparency in data handling. Given that the GDPR was rolled out for the EU and will be adopted by other regions in different scales, it is also important to realize that not all the protocols, procedures, and recommendations will apply to all governments. Interpretation is key, especially about exceptions to general rules. Consultations are mandatory with the local authorities and legal advisors to make sure that implementing the requirements of the GDPR are in line with local laws.

Impact of GDPR on Research

The research community was not spared from the effect of GDPR either. The legislation calls for transparency and accountability in research, especially by individuals who handle personal data. In research, GDPR provides guidelines to support archiving and research, in the process inculcating confidence and trust among the public and other participants in research. Regarding research, GDPR has the requirements outlined below.

Importance of Consent

GDPR recognizes the need for consent before individuals participate in research. Consent gives research an ethical outlook.

Participants are free to withdraw consent and their participation from the study if they feel something is not right. They also have control over the way their data will be applied throughout the research exercise. Consent is basically about building and maintaining public trust.

Public Interest

According to the GDPR, all research should be a matter of public interest. All research organizations must obtain, protect, and use the data collected in a prudent manner, whether the studies are conducted in their research facilities or even in learning institutions. Everything about research is a matter of public interest.

Data Storage

All the data that is obtained during research is critical and valuable. For this reason, it must be stored for future reference and use. The GDPR recognizes how important scientific research is to understanding some of the problems facing society today and that this data can be useful in solving problems in the future. Therefore, data must not be destroyed after the study is complete. It will be stored indefinitely. Irrespective of the initial reason or purpose for research, some datasets can be used for different research studies.

Meet the Principles of Good Practice

Any research conducted under the guidelines of the GDPR must meet specific good practice standards and protect the interests of all participants. The research systems must be secured and encrypted such that they cannot fall into the wrong hands, and even if they do, become useless to the hackers.

Impact of GDPR on Learning Institutions

GDPR replaced the Data Protection Act (DPA), changing the way learning institutions handle and manage information and data within their premises. Under the DPA, learning institutions are tasked with ensuring this data is protected and secure all the time. The GDPR, however, adds more responsibilities to the institutions. They must ensure that the information, irrespective of the form it is available in, is managed accordingly and complies with the new regulations. Institutions that do not comply with the new regulations risk fines of up to £500,000.

So, how does the GDPR affect schools? There may be several similarities between the DPA and the GDPR. However, most of the changes that institutions can expect relate to data handling. The following are some of the things that institutions will have to be on the lookout for.

Data Processors

It is now a criminal offence to work with a data processor or IT recycling partner that does not meet the required standards. Data processors must be accredited under ISO 27001 and other relevant asset disposal compliance rules. The institution must also make sure that they conduct checks and employ only accredited companies to dispose of their IT gadgets and assets at the end of their useful life.

Contracts

Under the DPA, learning institutions do not necessarily need to have a contract in place with their data processors. However, GDPR bestows a new requirement that all data processors must have a contract with the school. It is illegal to operate as a data processor without a service level agreement or a contract with the school.

Penalties

Penalties for non-compliance could see schools pay fines of up to £500,000 if they do not comply with GDPR requirements. The data controller might be liable for penalties of close to £20 million, along with anyone else who might have assisted them in operating within the school without the proper documentation. Simply put, you must follow the rules.

To prevent these fines and the risk of non-compliance, everyone who is involved in the learning environment must go back to the drawing board. In case you already meet the DPA regulations, you might be halfway there. Most of the requirements remain the same. You must, however, make sure you are compliant with GDPR.

Things will be relatively easier, given that most of the principles have not changed. In due diligence you must take precautions to make sure you have everything in check. All the key decision makers in the school must make sure that everyone who matters is aware of the change from DPA to GDPR. They must also be aware of the reasons for the change and the ramifications of these changes. The new legislation will definitely affect the schools, so all players must be aware of what it means to them.

The manner in which private and privacy information is communicated will also change. Schools must review their procedures and have a plan in place to make sure that they address all changes in time when the GDPR comes into effect. The penalties for non-compliance are unnecessary and avoidable, especially for procedures that are basically an upgrade from DPA.

Schools must also conduct information audits to understand the data they hold, learn about their students and personnel, and comprehend how this data is used. They must also be clear about where they obtain data from and how they use the data in their care.

Schools must go back to the drawing board and address the procedures in place for managing individuals' data. Everyone has a right to specific data access. The institutions must clearly state how they handle data, including deleting data from parties whose information is no longer relevant to the institution. On the same note, consent must take precedence. Institutions need a review on how they obtain data, who they ask for data, and whether they consent to the requests or not. They must also obtain consent from the relevant parties before they make any changes to the data.

Schools must have a data protection officer, and a similar requirement is expected of government agencies. The role of a data protection officer is to handle data protection compliance and make sure that they oversee all activities involving compliance in the institution. The data protection officer will also act as the main consultant and the go-to person for any issues regarding data access and protection.

There must be procedures in place to deal with and manage data breaches accordingly. Data breaches must be reported as and when they happen. The institution must also investigate the breach and present a credible report on the breach and steps that they are taking to prevent a similar situation in the future.

Impact of GDPR on Consumers

Too many data breaches were experienced in the recent past. Systems were hacked and consumer data was compromised. Most of the companies whose systems were compromised did not have a plan in place that addresses the risks of such hacks to their customers. Instead, most of them only focused on how they could get their businesses up and running and how to reduce the possible cost of litigation.

In the past, a lot of information has been exposed about consumers on the internet. In light of this, GDPR proposed a few changes that would allow consumers the right to understand how companies use their data. The companies must inform the consumers when their data is hacked and what the company is doing to resolve the situation.

In the aftermath of an attack, businesses must inform the relevant authorities within their mandate so that the affected customers can take personal measures to ensure that their data is not misused. This way, while the company is dealing with the problem from their end, the customer can also follow up to ensure that they are safe.

One of the important changes that GDPR brings about is allowing customers easy access to personal data than they had before. Customers wield more power over their data today. They can demand to be informed about how their data is used, how it is processed, and, more importantly, they can request details of how the information is implemented in a way they can understand.

Many businesses have already taken steps to make sure they comply with these requirements. Procedures and actions as basic as sending customers emails or text messages about how their data will be used are appreciated. In these messages, the company also includes an opt-out option so that if the customer does not wish to have their data used, they can revoke consent and cease to be a part of whatever program the company is running that needs their data.

In the retail industry, companies are reaching out to customers to request their approval to be included in the retail store databases. What is appealing about these decisions is that companies realize the importance of addressing and seeking consent from their customers. Without this, they risk hefty fines.

Gone are the days when customers would be bombarded with emails from companies, some which they can barely recognize. In those days, you would find your personal details on a mailing list that would keep sending you unsolicited emails. Today, thanks to GDPR, you can only appear on these lists if you give express consent to the company. You should also realize that consent can be withdrawn just as easily as it was given.

Businesses must now stay vigilant and make sure they operate without infringing on consumer rights to data protection and transparency. While a lot of companies are already sending correspondence to customers, there is the risk that hackers might take advantage of this and initiate phishing hacks, stealing vital customer information in the process. This is a bigger concern, especially when you consider the fact that customers are now receiving many more emails from companies than they used to. As companies rush to comply with these requirements, it is important to mention the need for customers to stay vigilant, too, lest they fall victim to unscrupulous users.

Impact of GDPR on Businesses

Given that the GDPR is already in effect, how can you make sure your business is ready for what lies ahead? For the most part, some businesses will need a complete overhaul if they are to stay competitive in the market. Other than the threats and fines for non-compliance, GDPR actually has a few goodies in store for business owners. It offers several avenues where businesses can take advantage and level the playing field, and for some, even scale the scope of their operations.

Improved Cyber Security

Cyber security concerns have been a thorny issue for businesses for a very long time. Given the sophistication in attacks and the need for resilient networks and systems, businesses are looking at the prospect of rethinking their strategies regarding cyber security. Through the GDPR recommendations, critical data will only be handled by a few people in the organization. On the same note, businesses are mandated to disclose any breach of personal data to the relevant authorities within 72 hours from the moment they realized they were hacked.

For businesses, such changes might seem too intense at the moment, but they will help them reduce the risk of attacks in the future, thereby providing a platform for improving data security and establishing a culture of compliance.

Data Management

Businesses must also review the way they manage data in their operations. Data audits will help them understand their current position regarding data access and management, in light of the current threat environment.

For businesses, creating the position of a data protection officer might come in handy, because they will be tasked with overseeing anything to do with data in the organization. However, they are not mandated to create this position, unlike schools and government agencies.

Improve Return on Investment

Once businesses can streamline their operational databases, it is easier to communicate their needs to customers and stakeholders so that they understand why the company is spending so much money on security appliances and systems. From here, they can also create marketing strategies that will help the shareholders understand the need for such spending and explain the prospective returns in the foreseeable future. This tackles the problem that has been persistent in the business world for a very long time - how to justify the net spending on improving security.

Implementing GDPR will definitely come with some challenges at first, but in the long run, the prospects are good for the future and for businesses that plan to stay competitive in a world whose technological advancements are evolving at a rapid pace. GDPR is expected to bring forth a wealth of opportunities for individuals, organizations, and businesses and to foster an element of transparency within the business environment.

Chapter 8

Embracing the Future of Cyber Security

If you could predict the future, would you want to live in it? Many people are amazed, if not bamboozled, by the current state of the digital environment. Change is inevitable. We must embrace it. If you see some of the amazing inventions that have been created over the past few years, you can almost look forward to the future with great anticipation and excitement. However, it would be a folly to imagine it will be all bliss.

Just as much as we look to the future, so do hackers and other cyber terrorists. Everyone is excited about new technology. As we explained in the fundamentals of cyber security, all technology is of dual use. It can be used for as much damage as it can be used for good deeds. What matters is whose hands the technology falls into, the resources they have at their disposal, and their intentions.

The amount of cloud services, IT systems, and connected devices keeps increasing, which is a good thing, as the more connected a network is, the more value it possesses. All these systems process unimaginable volumes of data, commonly referred to as "Big Data". We must do all we can to protect this information, lest it falls into the wrong hands. For a world that relies heavily on data analysis, bestowing the right data upon a powerful entity with the right resources and, at times, government backing can lead to disastrous results.

However, not all available data is too sensitive. With this argument, you are probably looking at data security from the point of your confidentiality. While this might be true, the truth is that you can never be too sure what someone does with your data. What you feel is not confidential might be a goldmine for someone else. You might feel the data is worthless, but someone else can use it to trace your location. That is vital information.

Future Cyber Threat Assessment

There is too much data online that can be exploited, digitized, and even weaponized. From individuals to organizations, a lot of people stand to gain a great amount by exploiting the vulnerabilities in your networks and devices. Given the rate at which technology is advancing, the perceived future threats relating to cyber security might fall into any of the categories noted below.

Espionage - Selling privileged information to an enemy is not just limited to inter-country spats; today, companies find themselves in a very tight spot, especially given the lengths at which competitors are willing to go to get an advantage in the market. Some of the information that is traded includes passwords, accounts, hospital records, and credit card details.

Other than that, espionage can also be used to access privileged information. In the scenario above, the goal is to get some money. The hacker obtains information and sells it. However, in this case, the hacker is looking for specific information. The end result might be bigger than the immediate financial benefit of having that information.

Kidnapping - Kidnapping in the digital sphere works in the same way traditional kidnapping works. The hackers intercept information that they deem important, encrypt it, and demand ransom from the owners or recipients to decrypt it for them. Organizations and businesses that handle critical information, such as hospitals, are some of the most common victims of these hacks.

Phishing - Phishing is almost the oldest trick in the book. Today, however, hackers who use this method have to go the extra mile to sell their agenda. Phishing emails are camouflaged to make you believe you are responding to an official email. However, the scam is to trap you into providing important information about yourself. Spear phishing is a directed phishing attack that is aimed at specific people, and their projected yield is very high for the hackers.

Intrusion - Intrusion can be performed for many reasons. Someone who has unwarranted access to your system might do a variety of things in the network. Intrusions can be geared towards specific and targeted damage or general damage. The hackers can also get inside the system and alter information, in the process making everyone else operate on disinformation.

DDoS - DDoS attacks are very common these days. In such an attack, a wide network of computers is programmed to overload a specific service or website with traffic such that nobody else can access it. DDoS attacks are primarily meant to cripple a website, a service, or a specific individual.

Consequences for the Average User

The world did not just go digital; it also went mobile. There is an amazing list of things that you can do with the data at your disposal. The ease with which you can conduct businesses using your phone is amazing. However, this also calls for heightened caution. If someone gains access to and controls your mobile devices, they can nearly control your entire life.

Think about everything they will have access to, from your social media accounts, your contact list, your messages, photos, videos, and any other information you might have on the device. Thus, you must take responsibility for your actions and try to protect your devices to the best of your abilities.

Most companies have information that is no longer only restricted to or accessible to system administrators, but also by an interconnected network, meaning that most people in the organization have access to that information. Companies are spending so much to safeguard their information. However, as an employee, you must also do your best to make sure you protect the information under your care.

Social engineering is one of the methods that hackers use to gain access to systems. The victims are unaware they are being targeted. Hackers take time to study their victims and understand the things they do, how they go about their lives, the things they like, and so forth. Social engineering hacks demand a lot of patience for the hacker to cultivate an approach that their victim will never suspect. By the time you are hacked or used to get into a privileged system, you will barely realize your role in the hack. If you do, it might be too late, since the hacker will have already disappeared, wiping all traces of their existence from your life.

Protecting the Internet of Things

Experts in the industry are currently well aware of the methods they can use to protect conventional devices like computers, smartphones, and other mobile devices. However, since we are venturing into uncertain waters with the internet of things, is everyone ready for the risks that they present? Think about home automation devices, thermostats, refrigerators, self-driving cars, and all the other amazing devices that are shaping the prospect of the future.

Security is mandatory to protect these devices. Hacking into any of these devices will definitely have extreme ramifications, not just for the user who was hacked, but also for the companies that build or maintain the devices. Effective controls must be built into such products, and they must also be passed through rigorous security testing to ensure they are ready and safe for deployment on a large scale.

Big Data

More and more devices are joining the internet each day. Whenever you purchase a new device, you try to connect it to other devices or systems you own, so that you can enjoy a seamless experience whenever you need to. More devices on networks means more data, whether structured or not.

Mobile adoption has been the heartbeat of the growth of social media over the years. With time, third parties realized they can leverage their services on social networks. They realized people want to play games, date, learn, and do so much more on social networks. They also realized the insane potential that lies therein, with all the data social networks already collect about their users.

Data scientists currently work closely with project development teams to help them understand what data they are accessing and what they can do with it to influence user behavior when interacting with their apps online. One of the pitfalls of this trend is that, while the companies say they collect your data to understand you better and help them build products and applications that can serve you better, what they actually do is use the data to manipulate you into doing whatever it is they please. The end game for most of these companies is the balance sheet. How much money are they making from manipulating you to do something? And what if such companies are hacked?

If they could manipulate you into decision making, imagine what a hacker could do with that information. Manipulation is not just a matter of clicking a few links online or swiping left and right on your phone. Manipulation is a science. Even the brain, independent of cyberspace, presents important data that researchers can analyze and use to understand human behavior. Some cyber criminals are part of an elaborate network that includes data scientists and researchers, and at times they operate with the backing of a foreign or local government. This is too much power to wield by a shady entity.

Big data is not just about presenting challenges in the form of cyber criminals. It is also a means through which security experts can protect the cyberspace. It takes a lot of planning to execute a cyberattack without leaving traces behind. Most of this is only possible in the movies. However, in the real world, it is still possible to do so, but the planning must be very intimate. Experts can use data patterns to understand their systems and networks better, and in the process, help them predict attacks before they are executed.

The sad bit is that it might take days for experts to comb through unstructured data, during which the hack might have been executed already. To mitigate this challenge, cognitive security is one feature that will be advanced into the future. Experts currently make use of machine learning to process data efficiently. This also gives them an accurate representation of data and the current security position.

Stringent Regulations

2018 was a significant year in cyber security. The number of data breaches that were reported were record-breaking. This was also the year the GDPR was implemented. There were many learning points from the events that transpired in 2018.

Companies, for example, were aware of and had more than two years to prepare for the GDPR. However, some took it lightly, and when the resolution was passed, they faced dire consequences barely a year later. About a month after the GDPR resolutions were passed, thousands of complaints were reported, an increase of more than 150 percent compared to a similar period in the previous year.

Issues were raised about GDPR before and after it was implemented. Many wondered whether companies could actually be held accountable for breaches. According to the regulation, companies that are found guilty are liable to fines of more than £16 million, or 4 percent of their turnover worldwide. Companies like Uber have learned the hard way that the GDPR is a serious matter.

Companies must be held accountable for managing and protecting the consumer data they receive. They must handle it carefully, or they'll face hefty fines. Companies like Facebook and WhatsApp have also found themselves in hot water with the GDPR. Data protection and responsibility is no longer a laughing matter.

In the broadest sense, GDPR is giving power back to the end user, but at the same time holding companies accountable for any information they request or retrieve from their users. They must protect this data or face the consequences. Sadly, most businesses are only doing the bare minimum to protect the information they have. Companies must encrypt all the data and efficiently manage keys and access control services. Encrypted data is largely useless to anyone who has it unless they have decryption protocols.

Quantum Computing

Crypto-agility has been touted as the future of cyber security. Crypto-agility is a discussion you will come across often as the masses embrace it. The threat to present security protocols become greater with the increase in computing power.

Through crypto-agility, businesses can use algorithms that are flexible such that they can change them without necessarily having to interfere with the system infrastructure, especially if the original encryption fails. What this means is that businesses have the power to protect their interests from threats that are yet to be actualized, like criminals who have harnessed the power of quantum computing before its time. As such, you no longer have to redo the entire security system every year in response to growing computing power.

Artificial Intelligence

The use of artificial intelligence (AI) is rather limited at the moment. However, with increasing computing power, the possibilities of using AI are limitless. There are rumors of a potential AI powered attack with the ability to power down an FTSE 100 company. If this is true, hackers could easily breach a system undetected and obtain as much information as they desire. They will also have time to study the systems and behaviors, adapt to the environment and finally unleash catastrophic attacks that could bring down companies.

AI might soon be implemented in chatbots to engineer unsuspecting victims to click dangerous links, through which their personal files and information are stolen. Hackers might also crack down on websites and applications that are not properly protected, inserting chatbots where they were non-existent.

Ransomware

Until 2017, not many people were aware of ransomware. The WannaCry outbreak and several other attacks that targeted high net worth individuals was just the beginning ("North Korea blamed for WannaCry, PoS attacks and Bitcoin phishing," 2018; Popli & Girdhar, 2017). The FBI believes that more than $1 billion has been paid as ransom to the attackers[27]. The ransomware is still in play, though the attacks are relatively subtle. However, experts believe that attackers might come back with a bolder move in the coming years.

---

[27] FBI Report on ransomware
https://money.cnn.com/2016/04/15/technology/ransomware-cyber-security/index.html

This ransomware attacked hundreds of thousands of computers in at least 150 countries. The hackers demand some money to unfreeze computers. Some of the key targets were hospitals, governments, and big companies. Russia, for example, was reported to be one of the hardest hit targets according to a report by Kaspersky Lab. Some of the victims included banks, railways, Russia's second largest mobile phone operator, Megafon, and the interior ministry.

In Germany, electronic boards at different stations that announce departures and arrivals were affected. However, German representatives do not believe their train services were affected.

Learning institutions in China were victims, too. Students had ransom pop-ups in their laptops, disrupting learning activities in most of the universities. Most learning institutions either use pirated computer software or outdated software, and as a result, students who access their facilities are equally at risk. Students were asked to pay $300 to gain access to their devices and resume working on their projects, most of which having deadlines that were almost due.

The western city of Chongqing struggled to process card payments at petrol stations because the China National Petroleum Corp was infected. In China alone, more than 30,000 businesses, individuals, and institutions were victims.

CJ CGV, the largest cinema chain in South Korea, was also hacked. Their advertisement servers that project to around 50 cinemas were hacked. Japan Computer Emergency Response Team Coordination Center, Hitachi, Dharmais Cancer Hospital in Indonesia, India State

Police, NHS in the UK, Telefonica in Spain, Renault in France, Nissan FedEx, and hospitals in Ireland were affected. This is how ransomware can cripple the world. Now imagine a situation where hackers target a country, crippling every important industry.

The interesting thing about the WannaCry ransomware attack is that it exploited a common Windows vulnerability that the NSA also exploits - EternalBlue. EternalBlue is an NSA exploit that was implemented on older Windows operating systems. Microsoft had created patches and released them earlier on to deal with this flaw. Most of those who were affected either ignored the patch or were using older Windows systems that were no longer supported. Through the Windows server message block protocol (SMB), harmful data packets can be sent to your device undetected. The hackers encrypted data in victims' machines, demanding ransom in Bitcoin.

Microsoft responded by releasing an emergency patch, helping them stop the attack within a few days. Further research also revealed a kill switch which stopped infected computers from echoing the infection to networks they were connected to. This attack was formally blamed on North Korea by Australia, the UK, and the US in December 2017.

Digital Transformation

Everyone talks about cloud computing or offering cloud services from time to time. Most companies and individuals are migrating their access to cloud service hosts. With most people migrating to the cloud, there is a need to carefully scrutinize the migration processes. Hackers understand that businesses are trying to cut down on operational costs and reduce or eliminate downtime. They could also take advantage of this and piggy-back the migration exercise, then attacking cloud providers and their customers from within.

Nation-State Attacks

Russia is notoriously culpable for targeted cyberattacks to achieve unknown larger objectives. A while back, the FBI revealed that more than half a million home office routers were infected by Sofacy group, a Russian threat actor. This breach also affected networks connected to storage devices all over the world, allowing the hackers enough room to control the systems remotely. Considering that most of the IoT devices are poorly protected, you can expect many other countries to jump on this bandwagon.

Data Weaponization

Did you know that your data and personal information can be used against you? This is a trend that has grown over the years and will only get worse as hackers become more sophisticated. Tech giants are doing their best to safeguard your information. However, are they really doing enough? Look at the case of Facebook, for example. They admitted to using private correspondence and personal data in their possession to generate profits to the tune of billions of dollars. When you like or follow certain brands on Facebook, you further volunteer some information about yourself.

This allows Facebook an in-depth look into your life, knowledge that becomes a treasure chest for the advertisers.

Facebook has also been accused of manipulating the moods of their users through an emotional contagion[28] experiment. Facebook was at the center of Cambridge Analytica's infamous election manipulation practices, as well. Imagine a social network so powerful it can use its data to influence elections in more than one sovereign country. Now, think about hackers wielding this much power; it might be chaotic.

Satellite Attacks
Satellite communications have interested several hack groups in the past. Symantec reported one such successful hack that targeted telecommunication companies in Southeast Asia, especially imaging and geospatial mapping companies. Satellite communications that the military, planes, and ships use to access the internet also have some vulnerabilities that can be exploited.

Some of these scenarios paint a grim picture of the future, but all is not lost yet. Experts believe that multi-factor authentication should be implemented by all businesses. A lot of businesses still use passwords as their only line of defense. Most companies and states have studied the GDPR legislation and are adopting versions of it that are relevant to their cause. In California, for example, as of the

---

[28] https://www.forbes.com/sites/gregorymcneal/2014/06/28/facebook-manipulated-user-news-feeds-to-create-emotional-contagion/#218a866839dc

year 2020, consumers can sue companies in the aftermath of a data breach. Breaches and vulnerabilities might be impossible to eliminate. However, we can do many things to avoid falling victims and improve our chances of preventing disaster.

Conclusion

No one is safe. Someone is always watching. These two statements might seem simple, but they hold more meaning than you may be aware. You must be vigilant in cyberspace if you are to stay safe. Hackers are always trawling the internet, hoping to pounce on any vulnerabilities in your system. What can you do about it? How should you go about it?

In truth, complete protection once you connect to the internet is a myth. No one can guarantee you with 100 percent certainty that they will protect your devices and networks completely. There is always room for error. You must be reasonable and admit this.

Like most communication networks, cyberspace can be used for good and bad deeds in the same manner. The elements that make it amazing and allow you to go about your business without a hitch are the same elements that make it a nightmare for others. Everyone enjoys convenient internet access. Hackers love it even more, because it allows them to use your resources against you.

The diversity of the digital world demands that you take extra precaution when managing your network. There is much at stake. Data security is not just about protecting financial data, but is also about protecting the consumption of records, disclosure, and implementing the necessary punitive measures to mitigate data loss. For a long time, many companies have not played their role in protecting consumer data. This leads to uncertainty when they are hacked.

A lot of organizations are finding themselves on the wrong end of legislation and under intense pressure to react in light of the dynamic increase in cyber threats. Cyber security is a battle that doesn't seem to have an end in sight. Hackers evolve just as much as the digital space does. For the most part, many of the problems we encounter in cyber security are as a result of the nature of the technology, complexity, and human influence, especially in terms of judging actions and information to determine whether they are safe.

In the foreseeable future, the same risks will still be imminent. However, they will probably be more complex, in light of the possibility of advanced cyber threats. We are looking at a future where artificial intelligence takes center stage. The internet of things will have come of age, and quantum computing will possibly be close to reality.

Each day, corporations work hard to come up with new defense mechanisms to mitigate older threats so that they never bother anyone again. However, hackers take this as a challenge to improve their systems. They adapt and come up with new tools and techniques to exploit vulnerabilities in different systems they come across.

The interesting thing about cyber security is that we cannot ignore it. Technology has become an integral part of our lives. There are so many things that we do today that would be unimaginable without technology. An outage in one sector might ground an entire country. Growth in IT systems and innovation is imminent, as are the threats that come with it.

Innovation breeds amazing technology. This technology is important in shaping the future of the world. At the same time, terrorists, hackers, and other criminals also see the benefits of this technology, albeit in a different perspective compared to the rest of us. As more people gain access to the internet, the possible victim scope widens, and the potential number of hackers also increases.

All hacks are not bad, however. As we have seen earlier, some hackers are good and we need them. These are white hat hackers. White hat hackers can be an important arsenal in your war chest. They help to monitor your network and devices and perform penetration hacks on your system, reporting back to you on the vulnerability of your network. Without these hackers, it would be almost impossible to preempt an attack or circumvent it.

Improving cyber security is not a one-off thing. This is a going concern that every involved party must be aware of. The moment you carry out a cyber security drive and rest easy assuming that everything is okay is the moment, your weakness is exposed. Remember that hackers are always working around the clock to adapt and beat the security patches released frequently. If hackers are not taking a break, why should you?

A lot of vendors have implemented security measures in their hardware and programs, to ensure that their users are protected. Most products we use today are more secure than similar versions from a few years ago. This is a sign that as technology changes, so does the need to boost security, and at the same time, ensuring the utility users derive from the products or services is not compromised. Without some of these efforts, the threats to cyber security would be unimaginable.

The ultimate issue concerning cyber security is not just about solving the cyber security problems, but how to manage them. These problems will always exist. The approach to cyber security is no different from what we do about drug abuse, hunger, crime, and terrorism. We can only manage them to the best of our ability. Depending on the scenario or environment, cyber security risks can lessen or worsen. Some attacks are opportunistic and simply take advantage of a victim that is down on their luck.

Most adversaries have more than one target victim. If the first one improves their systems before they strike, they fail and move on to the next victim. Therefore, cyberattacks might also be a matter of chance and opportunity. Adapting might be expensive, but it is a worthy investment.

We should strive to establish a culture of security where everyone involved in the life cycle of security systems plays an important role in protecting these systems. From the developers to the end users, everyone has a role to play in protecting their networks and systems. What this culture would bring to the fore is an environment where collaboration across the board is a reality.

If this were to pass, developer teams would come up with services and products that operate under specific guidelines to build security protocols into their services and products. This alone would help to improve the resilience of most systems and improve their functionality.

Security should not be implemented as an add-on. Instead, it should be featured at the core development level. Security must be an integral element in the basic design of computing architecture. Hardware and software must have security features implemented in their blueprints, instead of being implemented at the consumer level.

More importantly, end users need proper training and awareness of the risks they are exposed to. Most people fall victims to hacks not because they are vulnerable, but because they are ignorant of the status quo.

For organizations, businesses, and other entities, a risk assessment is mandatory if they are to survive the persistent cyber onslaughts. Management boards today hold more discussions about cyber security than ever before. This is a good thing, because they need assurances that their operations are fully compliant and understand the technological trends and the influence it has on their customers. Most of these discussions are held after receiving support from technology experts in the industry. Support can be offered in several ways but is aimed at improving the management decision processes and helping the decision makers create and implement new strategies.

We must also realize that technology serves as a driver of growth and business and as an enabler. While management will seek financial support to improve security or invest in some of the best security systems, they must also realize the value addition aspect of these decisions and the impact that such proposals will have on the business.

At this point in time, cyber security is almost a life calling. It is something you learn about from a young age, and you carry the lessons with you throughout your life. More devices will get connected to the internet in the future. All these devices are potentials for hacking. Does this mean that we should stop innovation for fear of hacking? No. The human race is a resilient species. We stand tall when faced by adversaries. We overcome. When we are beaten, we do not give up. We regroup, strategize, and come back stronger.

References

Fischer, J. E. (2005). *Dual-use technologies: inexorable progress, inseparable peril a report of the project on technology futures and global power, wealth, and conflict. CSIS series on technology futures and global power, wealth, and conflict.* Washington, D.C.: CSIS Press.

Forum, W. E. (2012). Rethinking Personal Data: Strengthening Trust.

Friedman, J., Metzler, I., Detmer, D., Selzer, D., & Meara, J. G. (2012). Health information technology, meaningful use criteria, and their effects on surgeons. *Bulletin of the American College of Surgeons, 97(7)*, 12–19.

Gujrathi, S. (2014). Heartbleed Bug: AnOpenSSL Heartbeat Vulnerability.

Guo, B. (2016). Why Hackers Become Crackers – An Analysis of Conflicts Faced by Hackers. *Public Administration Research, 5(1)*.

Gupta, S. (2019). *Ethical Hacking – Learning the Basics: Gain the Basic Concepts of Ethical Hacking.* Apress.

Hunter, D., & Huntert, D. (2003). Cyberspace as Place and the Tragedy of the Digital Anticommons Cyberspace as Place and the Tragedy of the Digital Anticommons, *91*.

Iagolnitzer, Y., Krzanik, P., & Susini, J.-F. (2013). Middleware for the Internet of Things: Standards. In *RFID and the Internet of Things: Chabanne/RFID and the Internet of Things* (pp. 217–243). John Wiley & Sons, Inc.

Kohl, U. (2015). Jurisdiction in cyberspace. In N. Tsagourias & R. Buchan, *Research Handbook on International Law and Cyberspace* (pp. 30–54). Edward Elgar Publishing.

Li, C. (2019). Defeat Man-in-the-Middle Attack. In C. Li & M. Qiu, *Reinforcement Learning for Cyber-Physical Systems: with Cybersecurity Case Studies* (pp. 189–204). Chapman and Hall/CRC.

Meredith, S. (2005). Offering flexible and remote working options at IBM. *Strategic HR Review, 5*(1).

Noor, S., Ahmed, M., Saqib, M. N., Abdullah-Al-Wadud, M., Islam, M. S., & Fazal-e-Amin. (2017). Ontology for Attack Detection: Semantic-Based Approach for Genomic Data Security. *Journal of Medical Imaging and Health Informatics, 7*(6).

North Korea blamed for WannaCry, PoS attacks and Bitcoin phishing. (2018). *Network Security, 2018*(1).

Popli, N. K., & Girdhar, A. (2017). WannaCry Malware Analysis. *MERI-Journal of Management & IT, 10*(2).

Sanchez, J. (2014). The NSA's Heartbleed Problem Is the Problem with the NSA.

See, M. R. (2003). The American Society for HIPAA* compliance presents: HIPAA SAP I, A HIPAA self-assessment program. *ACC Current Journal Review, 12(*3).

Smouter, K. (2018). The Year of the GDPR: THE YEAR OF THE GDPR. *Research World, 2018(*68).

Vegh, S. (2002). Hacktivists or Cyberterrorists? The Changing Media Discourse on Hacking. *First Monday, 7(*10).

Made in the USA
Columbia, SC
01 September 2019